FAST FREDDIE

MOTOR RACING PUBLICATIONS LTD
Unit 6, The Pilton Estate, 46 Pitlake, Croydon CRO 3RY, England

ISBN 0 947981 08 X
First published 1986

Photosetting by Tek-Art Ltd, West Wickham, Kent
Printed in Great Britain by Netherwood, Dalton & Co Ltd,
Bradley Mills, Huddersfield, West Yorkshire

FAST FREDDIE

DOUBLE WORLD CHAMPION FREDDIE SPENCER
THE MAN AND HIS MACHINES

Nick Harris & Peter Clifford
Foreword by Barry Sheene

MRP

About the authors:

Nick Harris has known Freddie Spencer throughout his international career. A former sports editor of *Motor Cycle Weekly*, he is now a freelance writer and broadcaster. British racing fans eagerly await his Grand Prix reports on BBC Radio Two.

Peter Clifford is a noted technical writer on motor cycle racing. An active racer himself, he is the author of *The Art and Science of Motor Cycle Road Racing* (Hazleton Publishing) and the editor of the respected annual *Motocourse*.

Consultant Editor of *Fast Freddie* is *Mick Woollett*, the only man to be, at different times, sports editor of *Motor Cycle News*, *Motor Cycling*, and *Motor Cycle* magazines and editor of *Motor Cycle* from 1976-1984.

Prominent among the photographic contributors are *Don Morley*, a former motor cycle racer who has won 16 national and international awards for his sports photography; *Leo Vogelzang*, a Dutch professional who specializes in Grand Prix racing and Leo's compatriot *Henk Keulemans*, an ardent bike racing enthusiast and follower of the World Championship scene.

Contents

THE MAN

THE MACHINES

Foreword

By Barry Sheene MBE
500cc World Champion
1976 & 1977

I'm delighted to be asked to write the foreword to Freddie's book because not only is he in my opinion the best rider I've ever seen but also a really nice guy.

His ability on the track while actually racing is clearly shown by his results and especially by his world championship double but it's also his knowledge of how to set a bike up that makes him so very special. He has built up a special relationship with Erv Kanemoto who worked with me for a season to learn all about the European Grand Prix scene a year before Freddie arrived. Freddie can tell Erv after each practice session just what is required to improve the lap times and this, coupled with his riding ability, has made him almost unbeatable.

I remember well his first appearance in Britain when he came over on the 750cc Yamaha and blitzed us all at the opening two races of the 1980 Transatlantic Trophy Series at Brands Hatch. I realized then he was something a bit special and he soon showed he had the ability to learn from his mistakes and to learn new circuits very quickly. He crashed in the third round of the series up at Oulton Park while leading and he has hardly ever made that sort of mistake since.

I also remember his first World Championship race on the NS500 three-cylinder Honda in the 1982 Argentine Grand Prix. We had a great race together with Kenny Roberts on the works Yamaha and he showed both Kenny and myself just what a threat he was going to be in the remaining 11 rounds that year.

Freddie displayed the determination to fight back when the chips are down when he won back that world 500cc title from Eddie Lawson after such a disappointing 1984 season.

Away from the track, some racers can think and talk about nothing else than racing and bikes. I've always found Freddie quite the opposite – intelligent and interesting to talk to away from the pressure in the paddock. Some people have said they find him a little aloof, but I've never found this – although perhaps he is a little shy with people he does not know.

The pressures on him while winning the two world titles in a year must have been enormous – I can still remember just how tough it was for me when I won my two 500cc championships. Freddie has coped brilliantly and I shall continue to follow his fortunes with great interest. I am sure there is more success to come. Believe me, it could not happen to a nicer guy.

Barry Sheene
Charlwood, 1986

FAST FREDDIE

THE MAN

By Nick Harris

A dream debut

European baptism, 1980

The steak and kidney pie lovingly prepared by the catering staff at the Kentagon, Brands Hatch, stayed firmly on the plate. The shocked 18-year-old just stared in amazement as his table companions tucked in. He turned to team-mate Richard Schlachter.

'You mean they put real kidneys in pies for people to eat over here?' he exclaimed.

Eighteen-year-old Frederick Burdette Spencer Junior had been out of the USA for the very first time for just 48 hours and was not finding it easy.

Outside, the sun was shining for once on a Good Friday Bank Holiday and over 50,000 fans had queued for miles down the dreaded A20 road from London.

It was time for the traditional opening two rounds of the 1980 Transatlantic Trophy, and with current world 500cc champion Kenny Roberts leading the Yanks and every Mum's favourite Barry Sheene captaining the Brits, nobody seemed too upset about the queues.

Back from his first brush with the delights of Brands Hatch cuisine, Freddie prepared for his first race in Europe. As he zipped up his blue and white leathers with an enormous number 8 emblazoned on his back, Concorde roared overhead leaving a white vapour trail in the blue sky pointing all the way back to the States.

It turned out to be a symbolic white trail high above the undulating Kent countryside for the lad from Shreveport, Louisiana.

He joined the rest of the star-studded cast on the lorry making its slow way round the demanding and picturesque 2.61-mile circuit. He stood at the back waving rather shyly to the crowd. After all, the men in front of him, joking and full of confidence, were known to millions of fans throughout the world.

From behind the chestnut paling fences the fans waved back to their heroes Roberts, Sheene, Haslam and Mamola and reached for their programmes to check on the identity of the lad at the back in those blue and white leathers.

Number 5 in the American team was Freddie Spencer, they read, nicknamed 'Fast Freddie' following successes in the States. Commentator Fred Clarke built him up with typical style.

'Fast Freddie Spencer making his debut in Europe and taking on the cream of road racing,' he barked to the assembled masses. Some made a mental note to check his progress. After all he had been fastest in practice on Erv Kanemoto's silver 750cc Yamaha despite some electrical problems. Others just carried on waving to their heroes, certain that nobody would win first time out in Europe against such star-studded opposition and dismissing his practice performance as a bit of a fluke. He would do very well just to finish in the first six in both races.

It took Freddie just three laps to make those doubters hastily reach for their well-thumbed programmes to check once again on the identity of the rider of bike number 5. By this time he was in complete control of the 13-lap race on

First race in Europe and 18-years-old Freddie Spencer guns his 750 Yamaha to a win at Brands Hatch during the 1980 Anglo-American Transatlantic Trophy series.

his very own silver bird, as the collective talents of Sheene, Roberts and New Zealander Graeme Crosby, riding the fearsome 653cc Suzuki, were left battling for second place.

The sporting British crowd rose to him at the finish as he stumbled back to the paddock. Surrounded by well-wishers and the persistent British press, sensing they had witnessed something a little bit special, he stuttered a few words before disappearing into the confines of the American camp, not really appreciating at that moment just what an impact he had made.

An hour and a half later, with all eyes firmly fixed on the silver fairing, he repeated his actions in the second leg. He didn't wait for three laps, but led from the start as the pack cranked into the frightening downhill Paddock Hill Bend. Once again he left the others, including team-mates Kenny Roberts and Randy Mamola, battling for second place as he reeled off 13 immaculate laps to take the chequered flag and spearhead the Americans' crushing victory in the series.

Over 4,000 miles away the sun was up and the town of Shreveport was just coming to life. Little did its population of around 250,000 realize that across the Atlantic, in a tiny corner of the garden of England far removed from Louisiana – a State steeped in the traditions and culture of America's deep South – that the 18-

Fast Freddie — as the fans saw him at Brands Hatch in April 1980.

The two men who have helped Freddie throughout his international career were with him when he made his European debut at Brands Hatch in 1980. Working on the 750 Yamaha he rode that day are, on the left technical wizard Erv Kanemoto, on the right, Iain 'Mac' Mackay.

year-old son of a grocery store owner had successfully climbed the first rung of a ladder that would make him the most famous son of their friendly city.

In the middle-class southern part of the city, his father and mother, Fred and June, waited for news of their son's first trip into the unknown.

For 12 years they had coaxed him along the road to stardom; watched him from retirement in his first-ever race on a 50cc Briggs and Stratton mini-bike when he was just six years old to domination of American racing and the verge of international stardom.

They, like the rest of the family, had given

him support and encouragement throughout those 12 hectic years. All those thousands of miles of travelling, late nights working on machines, running the store and keeping Freddie Junior's feet firmly on the ground, were worth every minute when they heard the news from Brands Hatch.

They probably knew long before any of us who saw his sensational European debut on that sunny afternoon that their son had the talent, determination and total belief in his own ability not only to become World Champion, but one of the greatest motorcycle racers of all time.

It did not take people in Europe very much longer to reach that same conclusion.

Freddie v Kenny

World Champion 1983

The stunned silence among the group of Yamaha personnel shifting their feet surrounding Kenny Roberts and his silent 500cc Yamaha was only punctuated by seething comments from the former world champion.

'Spencer went beserk on the last lap and put both of us in the dirt as he went up the inside on the right-hander at the end of the straight', he told the ever-growing group of journalists, mechanics and team manager Giacomo Agostini in the paddock at the drab Anderstorp circuit. 'He ran me off the track and I don't think he realized just what might have happened.'

Twenty minutes later on the victory rostrum he shook hands with Freddie and the air was cleared. Kenny was far more angry with himself than Freddie. He'd underestimated the determination of his great rival and he realized that one mistake had almost certainly cost him the chance of capturing a fourth world title

Just an hour earlier the pair of them sat side-by-side on the start line hunched over the tanks of their machines. The grid had been cleared and all they had left were their own private thoughts as they waited for the flag to drop on the 30-lap 1983 Swedish Grand Prix.

It was the penultimate event of the 12-round 1983 World Championship and tension was high, even among the usually rather staid Swedish crowd perched in the grandstands along the start-and-finish straight. Spencer's championship lead had been decimated to a paltry 2 points and Roberts had the scent of victory in his nostrils. After all, the former three-times World Champion had won the last three Grands Prix in Holland, Belgium and Great Britain and had pulled himself back from the dead after being a seemingly impossible 25 points adrift at one stage.

For 29 laps Freddie kept poking the front wheel of his NS500 Honda alongside Kenny without getting past and it was obvious the sparks were going to fly on the last lap.

Kenny pulled a massive wheelie going into the wide 160mph straight that doubles as the runway for the local airport, and as they braked for the crucial right-hander at the end, Freddie dived up the inside. Kenny had left his braking very, very late and as he laid his four-cylinder Yamaha into the bend he was forced wide by Freddie rushing down the inside and both riders found themselves careering down the grass at around 80mph. With that inside advantage Freddie was first to get back on terra firma and he negotiated the final bend with no such drama to take the chequered flag for the most important victory of his career.

No wonder Kenny was mad. He knew he was going to the final confrontation of the season at the Autodromo Dino Ferrari at Imola, near Bologna, in Italy 5 points adrift of Freddie, who could still finish second behind him in the race and clinch the world title. The split second he had underestimated the determination of his great rival had cost him dear. After all, if he'd

After a break of several years, the Italian Grand Prix returned to Monza in 1983. At the start, Spencer, on Honda no.3 to the extreme right of the picture, gets away on what proved to be a winning ride.

been in the same situation as Freddie as they braked he knew he would have done exactly the same thing.

If you are going to win a World Motorcycle Racing Championship there cannot be a better place than Italy to do it. Fair enough, you have to expect to be beseiged in the sample room of the Imola medical centre by thousands of fans for at least an hour after the race, with a police escort the only way back to the paddock. They love their racing and this final confrontation between the two Americans, one of whom was going to steal the world crown from their own hero Franco Uncini, had captured the imagination of the fans who had had to wait four long weeks since the fun and games in Sweden.

They bided their time by following the typical racing rumours that flowed during that period about who Yamaha would bring in to support Kenny. If he won the race and Freddie could only finish third they would tie on points, but Kenny would take the title because, although they would have won an equal number of Grands Prix, Kenny would have more second places.

The two gladiators flew home to Shreveport and Modesto, California to prepare for the battle that lay ahead round the 3.132-mile strip of tarmac that would do so much to determine their future. While playing golf, water-skiing and just relaxing they pondered on the outcome.

For Freddie, a World Championship victory would not only be a reward for 15 years of racing, but the springboard to launch him into the future. For Kenny, it marked the end of an incredible era during which he pioneered the path to Europe which Freddie, Randy Mamola and Eddie Lawson had followed so successfully. This was to be his last Grand Prix at the circuit where he had made his 500cc European debut nine years and three world titles earlier.

They flew back into a cauldron of excitement and tension. Yamaha brought in the Venezuelan World 250cc Champion Carlos Lavado to ride with Roberts and Lawson, but the fiery South American crashed in practice and broke his foot. So the scene was set for a head-to-head confrontation between the two rivals.

The 100,000 crowd went wild as Freddie

Dicing at close quarters at speeds up to 170 mph is a feature of modern Grand Prix racing. In the 1983 Italian Grand Prix, above, Kenny Roberts (Yamaha) leads Spencer (Honda), Randy Mamola (Honda, no.6) and Ron Haslam (Honda no.47) on one of the Monza straights, and below, Roberts, Spencer and Haslam crank into a chicane.

The battle continues. Above and below, Spencer leads Roberts in sunny Spain – a race that Kenny said later was the 'hardest of my life'. Spencer won this epic battle at the Jarama circuit by a bike's length.

Clincher – the San Marino Grand Prix at Imola and Spencer is on his way to his first World Championship astride the Honda NS500.

calmly walked up the start and finish straight at a gentle pace to straddle his NS500 Honda on the front row of the grid.

They clung to the high fences that surround the track and screamed their encouragement as Kenny, minus his helmet, slowly rode his red and white Marlboro Yamaha to pole position on the front row of the grid.

All the pent up frustrations of that long four-week wait erupted as the flag dropped on 25 laps of pure theatre which pushed the nerve of the two riders in centre stage to the very limit. Freddie knew one break in concentration or nerve would cost him dear against one of the all-time greats, who would try every trick in the book to break him down.

A good start was vital for Freddie and the battle plan looked good at the end of the first lap as he led past the pits, head down on the tank

with just the quickest of sideways glances at his pit board which told him his team-mate Marco Lucchinelli, with the fanatical support of the home fans, was keeping Kenny back in the third place. Behind him, Lawson was desperately trying to recover from a bad start. Then Kenny moved into second place and the real cold war started.

For four laps he kept moving alongside Freddie, showing him his front wheel without actually passing him, desperately trying to push him into making a mistake. Suddenly he switched the point of attack and took the lead on the long left-hand bend after the start. Almost immediately he slowed the pace, with Lawson carving his way through the pack and up into fourth place behind Lucchinelli.

Freddie would have nothing of it and snatched back the lead at the first chicane, only

Spencer (Honda, no.3) gets away alongside Roberts (Yamaha, no.4) at the start of the 1983 Austrian Grand Prix but later a broken crank put him out of the race – the only mechanical failure he suffered all year.

Easily identified. The unusual Italian Dainese leathers with the fox face motif on the back made champion-to-be Freddie easy to spot in 1983. Note his legs-out style as he corners.

Competitors do a lot of sitting and waiting during a Grand Prix – here Freddie waits patiently for his Honda NS500 to be readied at the Austrian Grand Prix.

After the disappointment in Austria came success in Yugoslavia. Freddie salutes the crowd after beating Randy Mamola (left) and Eddie Lawson (right).

for Kenny to regain it a lap later. The two rival pit crews were running the race like a giant game of chess, each trying to think one move ahead of the other and relay their plans by pit board to their two kings out on the track.

Eight laps from the finish Lawson at last squeezed past Lucchinelli and Kenny realized it was time for one more big effort. Once again he tried to slow the pace to give Lawson the chance to catch up, but once again Freddie replied and four laps from the end was back in front.

Time was running out for Kenny and he made his last desperate move by racing into the lead. He realized that despite a brave attempt Lawson was not going to catch Freddie and his championship was slipping away.

As the blue and white NS500 Honda's three cylinders chimed in symphony and Freddie, some 50 yards behind the flying Roberts, raced out of sight for the last time, all his pit crew could do was sit and wait – and pray.

The next 1min 50sec seemed like hours in the Honda camp. Then Freddie raced into view before braking for the final chicane, still some 50 yards behind Kenny's Yamaha.

21

Some just closed their eyes as he flicked first left and then right to negotiate the final hurdle. Nothing was going to stop him now and as Kenny saluted his ovation at the chequered flag Freddie, completely out of character, crossed the line with the front wheel of his Honda pawing the air. He was 500cc Champion of the World.

'As I accelerated out of the last corner towards the flag I knew I'd won the championship,' he told journalists at least an hour and a half after becoming the youngest rider to win the world 500cc title. After fighting

his way off the victory rostrum amid scenes of frenzied chaos he'd been required to give a urine sample in the medical room.

Once in there he found that giving the required amount took longer than riding the last five laps of the most important race of his life. When at last he'd satisfied the Italian doctors he found the building beseiged by thousands of fans who just wanted to shake hands with the new World Champion. Together with fiancée Sarie and a group of fellow riders, the new champion had to sit it out until more police arrived to clear the way for a hastily-organized press conference.

'Until that final bend I did not think about the championship because I was trying so hard to maintain my concentration,' he managed to explain before being rushed away in order to save himself and Sarie from being crushed.

Back in the garage Erv Kanemoto supervised the packing up of the team with his usual efficiency and with the air of somebody who had achieved a life-long ambition.

Freddie's championship win owed much to the polite and seemingly unflappable Californian with Japanese ancestry.

Their relationship goes far deeper than a rider and tuner and little could Freddie's father have realized in 1978, when he asked Erv to help his son, that a World Championship-winning partnership had been forged – or did

he? It was a brave step by Fred Senior to ask somebody to come in and take over the job he had been doing so successfully for 10 years. He knew he had done all he could and had set his son on the verge of stardom – the person taking over would have to be pretty special. Erv was well known in American racing circles where he had worked on a variety of two-stroke machines for former champion Gary Nixon, who had become a great favourite in Europe.

'I really appreciate the work that Dad put in from when I was six to until I was 16', explained Freddie Junior. 'What I appreciated even more was at the point he realized he'd done all he could for me as a tuner, he set out to find the best for me. My dad put his personal feelings aside because he only wanted the best for me and Erv was the best.'

160,000 spectators saw this battle of the giants at the 1983 Dutch TT at Assen, annually Holland's biggest sporting event. Here Spencer (Honda) leads, but challenger Roberts (Yamaha) went on to win.

Early race sort-out at the British Grand Prix at Silverstone with Spencer leading Mamola and the pack. Kenny Roberts was the winner of this race, on the aggregate of two parts after the first had been stopped following an accident.

Dramatic moment from 1983 Belgian Grand Prix as Kenny Roberts, battling to control his Yamaha, cuts inside Spencer (Honda) to take the lead.

Despite crashing on the last lap of their first event when the throttle of his 250cc Yamaha stuck open, the partnership blossomed and, as often 'happens, the pair have an almost telepathic understanding.

'Above all Erv is my friend,' continued Freddie. 'We have always got along real good and we understand each other perfectly. I trust him completely and he respects my riding. We communicate so well that when I come in

26

Vivid action as Freddie Spencer powers the Honda NS500 out of a corner during the 1983 Belgian Grand Prix.

during practice we hardly speak sometimes; we understand the situation just by looking at each other, by the expressions on our faces.'

'We think alike,' said Erv. 'We have a very similar outlook on life and racing. It's all about playing off strengths against weaknesses. One of Freddie's greatest strengths is his ability to say what is wrong with the machine. He doesn't have to spell it out, we think along the same lines, so if he tells me something I can fill in the rest of the picture. Freddie is also very good at compensating for a problem. You can see him working hard out there and he'll be going nearly

as fast with something wrong as he would with the bike right. That gives you a chance to put it right and make it a bit easier for him.'

Later on the day he won his first Championship, guests at a special celebratory dinner were kept waiting by the guests of honour, the new World Champion and Erv. Back in the hotel lobby, and out of sight of the banqueting hall, the pair of them were confusing the already very confused Italian telephone system from two tiny booths. Freddie was talking to Shreveport while, next door, Erv was telling the family back home in San Jose, in

Compact lines of the 1983 three-cylinder Honda NS500 are well shown in this shot from the Dutch TT as Spencer accelerates out of a corner.

California, about a rather special day a long way from home.

Little could Freddie have realized as he jetted back to Louisiana from Milan on an April morning earlier that year that the championship was going to turn into the best final-round head-to-head confrontation of the decade.

Who could blame him if his thoughts were more on the fortunes of the college basketball team and the family as he landed at home? After all, he had just opened up a massive 25-point lead in the championship over Kenny Roberts and his own team-mate Ron Haslam after the three opening rounds. He had completely recovered from the broken collarbone he sustained at the end of the 1982 season and a betting man would have shied away from any odds being offered on him not winning Honda their first-ever World 500cc Championship.

From the second lap in the opening round at Kyalami, in South Africa, when he snatched the lead in the sunshine, there was not much doubt that Honda had done their homework in the winter. He powered away for an effortless victory while Kenny had to battle for his second place and was far from happy with the performance of the new V4 Yamaha.

There could not have been a greater contrast in the weather for the second round at the Bugatti circuit at Le Mans, in France, which can be a very cold spot at the beginning of April. The bitter weather made it a pretty miserable place, and when Japanese rider Iwao Ishokawa was killed in practice and Swiss ace Michel Frutschi in the 500cc race, paddock morale hit rock bottom, especially in the Yamaha and Suzuki camps.

Freddie took an early lead in the 500cc event,

Above: Freddie glances behind during his battle with Roberts in the 1983 British Grand Prix. Below: Stars and stripes supreme. Freddie Spencer (centre), Kenny Roberts (left), and Randy Mamola display 'Old Glory' at the San Marino Grand Prix. They finished first, second and third in the 1983 500cc World Championship.

The decisive battle of the 1983 season took place in Sweden — here Roberts leads but Spencer is pushing hard and went on to win after a dramatic last lap incident.

The faces tell the tale! A grim looking Kenny Roberts (left) realises the title is slipping from his grasp as Spencer waves to the crowd after winning the 1983 Swedish Grand Prix. With them is third-placed Takazumi Katayama.

Unusual shot as Kenny Roberts (Yamaha) and Freddie Spencer (Honda) flip-flop their machines through a chicane during the 1983 San Marino Grand Prix at Imola.

but on the seventh lap of the 29-lap race Kenny took over and for five laps put some distance between himself and the Honda. Then disaster struck. One of his exhaust pipes split and he could do nothing as Freddie powered back in front, setting a new lap record in the process while collecting his second successive Grand Prix victory of the season. A bitterly disappointed Kenny limped home in fourth place behind the Hondas of Haslam and Lucchinelli. Even worse was to follow for him three weeks later in Italy.

The famous Monza circuit in a giant park on the outskirts of Milan has seen better days, but it played host to a fabulous race featuring as many twists of fate and fortune as an opera at La Scala just up the road.

When the dust had settled Freddie had scored another 15 points after a faultless ride while Kenny went off pointless to compete in the Transatlantic Trophy in Britain.

He had led the race unable to shake off his shadow Freddie and just three laps from the finish ran off the track into the gravel while lapping a backmarker, leaving Freddie free to pick up another maximum. Somehow, while in the gravel, he managed to keep the Yamaha's engine running and he rejoined the race in

Nearly there. Spencer heads for second place and the World Championship at the 1983 San Marino Grand Prix.

Rival's eye view of Freddie Spencer as he powers his NS500 Honda around a turn at Imola.

fourth place, only to run out of petrol on the last lap!

Kenny was never a person to hide his fellings and with Freddie seemingly cruising towards the title he was typically blunt on the eve of the fourth round at the very fast Hockenheim circuit, in West Germany.

'If we don't get a result here we can almost forget about the season and pack up and go home,' he told the assembled press.

He duly got his victory, but only clawed back 7 world championship points. Freddie finished fourth, unlucky in one respect, but very lucky in another. He was comfortably leading the race

and Kenny was thinking about his earlier promise when the ominous cackle of a split exhaust pipe echoed round the packed stadium which housed 100,000 fans. On the ailing NS500 Freddie began to drop back and was about to be overtaken by a group of four riders when the heavens opened and a monumental cloudburst fell on the 4.22-mile circuit. The race had to be stopped and the results stood because the required number of laps had been run.

Two weeks later at Jarama, in the dusty outskirts of Madrid, Kenny fought a duel in the sun with Freddie in a race so gripping that those who saw it will probably never tire of recalling it to anyone who will listen. In the energy-sapping heat the two of them fought a fearsome duel with no quarter asked or given. It was a classic encounter. They constantly swapped the lead, and with tyres fading in the heat they slid on and off the track, never more than a couple of yards apart. After 76 miles of frenzied action Freddie, with a superhuman last lap, took the flag by a couple of bike's lengths and was totally exhausted by his efforts.

'That was the hardest race of my life,' he said at the finish. Kenny was complimentary to his rival even in defeat:

Champion at last! Freddie Spencer gives a wave of relief as he crosses the line at the end of the 1983 San Marino Grand Prix. Although beaten by Roberts (who can be seen ahead) Spencer had finally outpointed his rival.

'I have to say that is the hardest I've seen somebody ride to beat me,' he confided. 'He was tired, really tired, but he still rode one hell of a last lap.'

The pendulum then began swaying away from Freddie and a week later, at the frighteningly quick Salzburgring, in Austria, he could only sit and watch Kenny cruise to victory. At the end of the 12th lap his crankshaft had broken and his championship lead was down to 6 points.

Freddie was back in the winning vein at the seventh round at the Rijeka Autodromo, some 10 miles inland from the Adriatic coastline, just over the Italian border in Yugoslavia. He led the race from start to finish and interest focused on one of Roberts' greatest rides. His Yamaha would not fire at the start of the race and he was over 20 seconds behind the last rider when he finally screamed away from the grid.

He ripped through the backmarkers like a scalded cat and fought his way into fourth place behind team-mate Lawson. The Honda camp waited for Lawson to slow sufficiently to allow the championship contender to pass and gain an extra 2 championship points, but with no orders from the Yamaha pit, Eddie just carried on. At the finish Kenny was furious, and how important those 2 lost points turned out in the final reckoning!

The Dutch TT at Assen is one of the biggest sporting events in the whole of Europe, and over 160,000 fans turned up to see the Spencer/Roberts confrontation for themselves although it was being televised live throughout Europe. Sadly, the race was marred by the appalling crash of Italy's reigning World Champion Franco Uncini, who, amazingly, was back in action the next season. It also turned into a bad day for Freddie, who had taken an early lead, but was soon under pressure from Roberts.

'We made the wrong selection of tyres,' he recalled. 'The problem wasn't evident in practice, but in the race the tyres were sticking so well my frame would flex under acceleration, causing the bike to skip.'

He dropped to third place behind Roberts and his Honda team-mate Takazumi Katayama, who did not get or expect any team orders from the Honda pit to slow and allow Spencer into second place.

The gap was down to 8 points as they made the short trip to Belgium and the magnificent Spa-Francorchamps circuit on which, 12 months earlier, Freddie had achieved his first-ever Grand Prix victory.

But there was no such victory celebration this time round as the dreaded tyre problem struck again after he'd taken an early lead. Fred Senior, who'd been brought over on Concorde by his son, could only sit and watch in dismay as Kenny pegged back Freddie's lead. With the front end of his Honda sliding the whole time he could do nothing as Kenny dived inside him at La Source hairpin, although coming out, the Yamaha slewed across the track and almost brought them both down.

'It's the most hopeless feeling in the world watching Kenny race away at the front and not being able to do anything about it,' he said to Dad back in his motorhome. 'I don't want it to happen again.'

Freddie went home with Dad with a whole month to kill before the next round at the Silverstone circuit, in Britain. He did all the usual things and relaxed, although with his lead slashed to just 5 points the nagging doubts were there.

Kenny was back to his cocky best and raced at

A hug from fiancée Sarie as she salutes the new World Champion.

Helmet off and on his way to the rostrum Freddie Spencer signals his joy at winning the 1983 500cc World Championship.

Laguna Seca, in California, and won before arriving at Silverstone full of confidence in his own and Yamaha's ability to win at the fast, flat circuit near Northampton.

His confidence was well-founded and he duly collected another valuable 15 points in controversial and tragic circumstances. Again Freddie took the early lead, but Kenny was in front when the race was stopped following the tragic deaths of Norman Brown and Peter Huber. Confusion reigned after the accident, with the leading riders not knowing if the race had been stopped. Eventually the red flag was shown and the riders had to complete a second 23-lap race with the placings from both races

deciding the winner. Kenny cruised away in the second leg and was an easy aggregate winner.

Freddie had suffered a broken piston ring in the second race and could only finish fourth behind Mamola and Lawson. All three riders' positions in both races added up to six points, making them joint second, but Freddie claimed that place and the vital 12 world championship points by just nine-hundredths of a second on overall time, which decided their placings.

He took time off before flying to Sweden with that precious 2-point lead, staying at the world-famous Hyde Park Hilton Hotel, in London. By the time he arrived at Anderstorp he was ready for the two most important races of his life . . . .

Down home

Racing's a family affair

It was just like the old days in the pits at one of the most famous mile-long dirt-track ovals in the world, San Jose, California.

There is no finer sight or sound in motor racing than that of a 750cc four-stroke monster being slid feet-up through a turn at well over 100mph and two spectators in particular were loving every minute of the action on the warm October evening in 1985.

Freddie Spencer had already tried to borrow a set of racing leathers to get out and join the action on the other side of the fence. Just because he was double World Road Racing Champion and still limping after damaging his ankle following a crash in Japan, did not enter into it. The fact he had not signed on and, tactfully, no leathers could be found to fit, prevented his appearance. Three-times World Road Racing Champion Kenny Roberts stood alongside him shouting encouragement to the riders going to the line for the final.

Long before the pair of them blazed the trail to Europe, conquering all before them to bring about a total American domination of the World Road Racing Championships – for so long the domain of European riders – they had been brought up in the rough, tough and super-competitive world of dirt-track racing. They knew that the grounding and education they had received on the crushed limestone, granite and clay surfaces had more to do with their world-wide success than any other single factor. They were back among their roots.

Shreveport is a friendly little city in the north-west corner of the Southern State of Louisiana. Fred and June Spencer were typical of the hard-working, strict baptist population. They lived in a relatively middle-class neighbourhood in a three-bedroomed house with a swimming pool, while the grocery store they ran was in the poorer north side of town.

Long before Freddie Junior was born on December 20, 1961 the family's one great diversion from their strict and orderly way of life was racing and speed. Fred Senior had raced cars, bikes and karts and it was no great surprise when their three children followed suit.

Daughter Linda raced karts and older brother Danny and Fred Senior raced bikes together. Dad stopped when Danny turned professional, and Danny stopped when he got married. The stage was set for young Freddie to follow in their wheel-tracks, although he was never pushed or persuaded because that was not the Spencer's way of doing things.

'The great thing about Dad was that he supported me but never pushed me,' recalled Freddie. 'He always allowed me to make my own decision and trusted my judgment. He always said even in my young days that if you stop enjoying yourself you can quit at any time.'

He also instilled a hard cutting edge into his son's attitude to racing which has been so evident during his World Championship campaigns.

By the time he was nine, Freddie was a regular winner and in 1970 took the Texas and Oklahoma Mini-bike Championships. Here the seemingly frail kid from Shreveport poses with his trophies in the crowded pit area of a Southern dirt-track.

'"Always remember that the person who is best prepared is the one most likely to win," he used to tell me at the beginning of each season,' continued Freddie, '"If you don't go out and practice there is a good chance you are going to lose." He knew how bad I hated to lose and I think he hated to lose too.'

Mother's influence was also enormous, providing the perfect balance of support to both Freddies as they travelled the length and breadth of the States in search of success.

'Mum's input was not only her support, but her insistence that I got a good education, so there was a good balance between the two. I also wanted a good education and so they never had to push or force me. I've always done what I wanted to do.'

From Monday to Friday Freddie led the same life as millions of young Americans during their early years at their local school. It was only when the school bell rang at the end of lessons on Friday afternoon that the usual routine went right out of the window.

'My elementary years from first to sixth grade I went to a school right down the street,' he recalled. 'They were good years for me. I played

American-style football and baseball, like a whole lot of kids. Then on Friday afternoons Dad would pick me up and we'd go to Dallas and race Friday night, Saturday night and then sometimes road race on the Sunday, and I'd be back at school on Monday mornings.'

From the moment Freddie competed in his first race when just six-years old on a 50cc Briggs and Stratton mini-bike there was no time for holidays in the Spencer household. No time because every spare minute away from school and the grocery shop was taken up with racing. He would spend at least a couple of hours a day practising on a couple of acres of land surrounding their house. He was soon riding a 50cc Honda mini-bike on which he scored his first win and by the time he was nine he was regularly competing on both 100 and 125cc Yamahas.

He was the Texas and Oklahoma Mini-bike Champion in 1970, and in 1972 he added three more State Championship titles to his collection. He won 83 races out of 90 entered and a local race report summed him up: 'Little Freddie Spencer is only 11 years old, 80 pounds and 4 feet 8 inches tall, but goes like a mini-Kenny Roberts on the track.' Prophetic indeed!

Fred Senior ran the show. He drove his son thousands of miles, maintained the bikes and managed the grocery shop during the week.

'If I drove a thousand miles I didn't want the bikes to break,' he explained. 'Not always having the fastest bike made him a good rider. We once drove from Shreveport to Benton, Arkansas, and to Sharpburg, North Carolina. It was about five in the morning and I'd had it, and so I let Freddie, who was 13 at the time, drive. We got there; I don't know how, but we got there. And what happened when we arrived? We made two laps and the chain came off because of frame flex.'

At home, young Freddie was determined to do well at school. He has always disliked criticism and although by the time he was eight and he had decided he wanted to be a professional racer he was determined that he would not let his school work suffer.

'I've always been very sensitive to criticism when it comes to anything I do personally, and school was the same,' he recalled. 'I never wanted to be called up in front of the class and asked "Freddie, have you done your homework?" and have to say "No", and then everybody would laugh. Also, everybody knew I raced and so school was very important to me, because people would say "What are you going to do when you grow up?" I would always say there was a good chance that I would race and they would reply: "But I mean, how are you going to make a living?" I never wanted to be

Freddie started road racing when he was 11 and first raced at Daytona in 1974 when he was just 13 years old. Here, aged 15, he tries out one of the then-new mono-shock 250 Yamahas.

39

accused of throwing my life away because they didn't understand racing. Because there was little racing in our area we always raced in other parts such as Dallas and places, and they really didn't understand.'

While his school-mates might not have appreciated just why he wanted to be a professional racer it was pretty evident to fellow competitors and spectators at the tracks just why he had such an ambition. And when the 'cherrrypickers' came down South hoping to earn easy money, they made note of his name for he often cost them a great deal of cash.

'From the age of six to 16 I was learning all the time', he recalled. 'I was riding mini-bikes up until I was eight and then I switched to a real motorcycle – a 100cc Yamaha. Up to 11, I rode 100 or 120cc Yamaha dirt bikes and when I was 12 it was a proper 250cc flat-tracker. Most of the professionals were using Bultacos at the time and I would get the opportunity to race against them in what we called outlaw races. These were unsanctioned, on quarter-mile oval tracks mainly in the South. The professionals would come down and do what they called "cherrypicking" where they could pick up some easy money, say between 200 to 300 dollars. Well, we made it very difficult for them. I guess you could say that a lot of the time I would beat them. Then they'd go off back to their world, which at the time I thought was a little unfair because they could come and race with us and I could beat them, but I couldn't go and be professional and race them on their home ground because I was not old enough.'

While dreaming of becoming a professional dirt-track rider, 11-year-old Freddie was in the pits at Dallas one Friday night when an announcement over the PA changed the complete course of his career, and probably his life.

'I was about to go out at Dallas and ride in the 100cc class when they announced over the loudspeaker that on Sunday, at Green Valley Raceway, just outside Dallas, they were going to hold a road race.'

He continued, 'It seemed like a perfect opportunity to try this out and so we spoke to the local dealer, who loaned us a 100cc Yamaha twin to race in the 250cc Production class, and

we went out the next day.'

It did not turn into a very auspicious beginning to a career that reached the dizzy heights of World Championship stardom, but it gave Freddie the first taste of road racing and he was hooked.

'It was raining, so I thought maybe I'll tell Dad "Let's go home," but he said they would race in this stuff and so I went out there and got dead last,' explained Freddie with a grin. 'The first thing I said when I got back was we have got to get something more competitive because I was 500 yards behind before we ever got into the first corner. It wasn't a bad experience and although the bike was not competitive it was a good thing I rode it. The big thing was that it wasn't something that I was scared of. I think so many people are nowadays. They get on a machine that's really too much for them and they go out and they don't learn any technique. I just went out and rode it and there was no pressure to win. That's the way Dad and I were and we just went out to have a little fun to see if I liked it.'

He certainly liked it, which meant more work for Dad and more time off school. Typically, he kept up his school work, found a real ally in his headmaster, and somehow still fitted in time to play other sports very successfully.

'For seven years I went to the Grawood Christian Academy, and the best thing about it was the principal, Mr Nichols, who was a real neat guy. Once I started road racing I was having to take more and more time off. I would be away on Thanksgiving and sometimes miss Friday and Monday because we started to go farther and farther away. He would agree I was excused absence, but always made sure I picked up the work I missed while checking on how I was getting on with my racing. I thank him for that because it was his support and belief in me that has been such a key factor in my life.'

'In both Junior and High School I played football, basketball and baseball. In my last two years at High School we reached the finals of the State Basketball Championship. In fact the most nervous I've ever been was when I started in my junior year in the State Championship semi-finals. I was in Shreveport, all my friends were there and I was more nervous than I've

Learning his trade – a very young Freddie Spencer dirt-tracking in America when World Championships were just a dream.

ever been doing anything else, including the World Championship races and I remember that feeling now and it was pretty good.'

At weekends he was riding in dirt-track and road races in the very competitive Western-Eastern Road Racing Association Championships and the journeys and time away from Shreveport got longer and longer.

'We were doubling up most weekends. We'd dirt track on Friday night and then go road racing at the Southwest Airport on Saturday afternoon and on Saturday night I'd be on the dirt again at Buffalo Speedway, which is about 40 minutes away. I did that pretty much through until I was 15 in 1977, when I started concentrating more on road racing.'

In 1974 he competed at the world-famous Daytona Speedway, on the Florida coastline, and after retiring in the 125cc race, which he was leading when his chain broke, he saw the

European Grand Prix stars in action for the first time.

Little could he have realized as he watched Italian World Champion Giacomo Agostini win the 200-Miler on his Yamaha that nine years later he would win the world 500cc title after a titanic battle with Kenny Roberts, who was riding in Agostini's team.

He enjoyed the competition and the camaraderie in the road racing paddocks that reminded him much of dirt-track racing, and more and more he concentrated his efforts and time into racing on tarmac.

'I think I was ready for a change because that is part of my nature. I'd been dirt-tracking all the time and I liked trying new things,' he explained. 'It was at the point where it was difficult for me just to do one thing. So the road racing thing was neat. Riding in one class was OK and then two classes, and pretty soon I was riding three, four, then five, and I wanted it all. Often I would have to ride my 400cc Yamaha against the 750s, but I'd just try a little harder.'

'The last year before I turned professional in 1978 I rode a Production 400cc Yamaha, a 250cc Yamaha, a 125cc Honda, a 750cc Suzuki and a 400cc Yamaha Cafe Racer in one afternoon of racing and I would jump from one machine to another without taking off my helmet.'

'At times I would also ride a TZ750 Yamaha. We just bought it out of the blue one day and I rode it and won on it, first race. Dad was taxed, if you know what I mean, trying to run the business – although Mum was helping him do that – in the day and then working on the dirt-track and road-racing bikes at night, plus driving thousands of miles at the weekends. We were in that situation from the time I was 13, just waiting for me to turn professional, and I was getting as much experience doing

everything I could. I even rode a 750cc Triumph on the dirt when I was 14 against the professionals.'

At the end of 1977 he held four class titles and at last was old enough to turn professional. He started his career where he had left off by winning his first race on a 250cc Yamaha at Daytona.

Gary van Voorhis of *Cycle News* had covered the professional racing scene for the last 12 years and was clearly impressed with the performance of 16-year-old Spencer and started his report thus: 'Freddie Spencer, current holder of four WERRA class titles and over 400 career pavement victories, began his AMA professional career today with a 76-mile romp that left the rest of the Novice field gasping for horsepower before the first lap was complete.'

Freddie won every round of the AMA Novice Road Race Championship that year apart from

CLASS 2—101cc to 125cc
Black Plates with White Numbers

No.	Rider and Home	Machine
2	Steve Gill, Sylvester, Ga.	Yamaha
3	Douglas Wilson, Rochester, Mich.	Yamaha
7	Virginia Durfee, Maxatawny, Pa.	Yamaha
8	Robert Wilson, Sr., Rochester, Mich.	Yamaha
9	Fred Veator, Warner Robins, Ga.	Penton
11	Clifford Guild, Jr., Timonium, Md.	Harley-Davidson
14	Barry Taylor, Griffin, Ga.	Yamaha
16	Al Nowocinski, Garden Grove, Calif.	Yamaha
17	Freddie Spencer, Shreveport, La.	Yamaha
18	Nicky Berman, Hollywood, Fla.	Yamaha
19	Dieter Guttner, St. Clair Shores, Mich.	Yamaha
20	Eddie Robinson, Knightdale, N. C.	Yamaha
21	Terry G. Poovey, Austin, Tex.	Yamaha
22	William Burbank, Asheville, N. C.	Yamaha
23	Robert Root, Riverdale, Ga.	Yamaha
24	Dewey Shelnutt, Fairburn, Ga.	Yamaha
26	Edward Green, Mansfield, Tex.	Suzuki
27	Gary Little, Titusville, Fla.	Yamaha
28	Chester Harvey, Tampa, Fla.	Yamaha
33	Allan Laabs, Riviera Beach, Fla.	Yamaha
35	George Wehrmeyer, Niagara Falls, N. Y.	Yamaha
36	Lloyd M. Graham, Knoxville, Tenn.	Yamaha
40	Ken Woodworth, Robinson, Ill.	Yamaha
41	Craig Gindele, Pittsburgh, Pa.	Yamaha
45	Kevin Deal, Miami, Fla.	Yamaha
48	Dr. Peter Frank, Philadelphia, Pa.	Yamaha
49	Robert Jacoby, Miss. State, Miss.	Yamaha
51	Henry Olynger, Jr., Marion, Ind.	Yamaha

Entry list from 1974 Daytona programme shows that Freddie Spencer from Shreveport, La. rode a Yamaha in Class 2 – 101cc to 125cc .... at the age of 13 years and three months!

Power-sliding a 750cc Honda dirt-tracker, Freddie Spencer leads the field on a half-mile track in California. It is this skill that has given him, and other American top-liners, the edge in Grand Prix racing in recent years.

Sears Point, when he retired with a loose exhaust pipe on his Yamaha. Yet he still found time to collect enough points on the dirt to win Junior status the following season.

'I'd concentrated on winning the novice road race series on my Yamaha and wanted 40 points on the dirt-track to become a Junior. On my 250cc Suzuki I raced a couple of times in Dallas and won and then went to Kansas for four or five races. I won all of them, which gave me just enough points.'

At the end of the season Fred Senior took the brave decision that he had reached the point where he could do little more to help his son, and he approached Erv Kanemoto to look after the team. It was a master stroke which had much to do with the World Championship success that was to follow.

'It was a very big decision for my Dad because he realized he was at the end of his ability to give me the equipment I needed to win or go on,' explained Freddie. 'He has never complained about it or interfered and I appreciate and admire him for that more and more every day as the years go by. He respected Erv not only for his ability to give me his best

equipment and his technical experience, but also because of Erv's nature and him just being a good man and a good influence on me. He trusted him with his son and our relationship together started out so good because Erv never felt he was taking the place of my father. He had my Dad's approval and that meant a lot to Erv.'

It was obvious from the start that the partnership was going places and after finishing second to Skip Aksland in the 100-mile Lightweight race at Daytona, when mechanical problems dropped him from the lead, he dominated 250cc racing in the States on the Howard Racing-sponsored Yamaha. In the Daytona race, despite finishing second, he beat later World Champions Toni Mang and Eddie Lawson. He was AMA 250cc Expert Champion after wins at Loudon, Sears Point and Laguna Seca. He also rode a Kawasaki Superbike to victory at the latter two races while still riding on the dirt on a Harley-Davidson XR750 with which he won 26 races on half-mile and one-mile tracks.

He was just a 17-year-old college boy who had never been out of the States when, at the end of the 1979 season, instead of having to

End of his apprenticeship –
Freddie Spencer rides a
CB750F at Daytona in 1980
as a member of the
American Honda team.

worry about college grades and basketball
results, he had to make decisions that would
have a bearing on the rest of his life. He could
ride for Honda, Yamaha or Kawasaki and he
could travel the world. Or stay at home.

Contract with Honda

The plan develops

There was a great deal of discussion in both the Spencer and Kanemoto households during the winter of 1979. They centered on three offers from the factory teams of Honda, Yamaha and Kawasaki. Honda wanted Freddie to stay in the States to race Superbikes with the promise of Grand Prix racing in a couple of years. Kawasaki were delighted with his two victories on their Superbike that year and wanted him to continue, while Yamaha had secretly made contact, offering him the chance to ride in the 500cc World Championship. Also he was considering riding Erv's 250cc Yamaha in either the proposed World Series or the World Championship.

'It was tough at the time. I'd graduated to Expert in both road racing and dirt-track and I had a bunch of choices,' he recalled. 'For somebody who was 17 years old and never been out of the States it was important that Erv was happy too and doing something he wanted to do. There were a lot of things to consider because there were a lot of other people involved, as well as my personal life and the financial aspect of it. Nobody really knows that Yamaha approached us about riding in the 500cc World Championship and there was no doubt about it – if we were to go we felt we would be competitive. The World Series didn't happen and at first I leaned towards riding for Kawasaki because I felt comfortable with them and I knew the bike would work well. We shied away from the World Championship deal with Yamaha, but at the time Honda were experimenting with a dirt-track bike. It was the one thing they had over Kawasaki, together with the money. I wanted to be paid well, so I talked to racing director Dennis McKay, and in December I made up my mind. I thanked Kawasaki very much for their offer, which I appreciated, but told them I was going to ride Honda.'

Part of the deal was that Freddie was allowed to race Erv's 750cc Yamaha both in the Daytona 200-Miler and in the Transatlantic Trophy races in Britain over the Easter weekend.

He almost gained Erv his first win in the prestigious 1980 200-mile race round the famous Florida speed-bowl, but just 12 laps from the finish the crankshaft broke while he held a one-minute lead, letting Frenchman Patrick Pons through to win. Two days earlier Freddie had made a good debut on the 1,000cc Honda Superbike in the 100-mile Superbike race, finishing second to New Zealander Graeme Crosby (Suzuki) and just 24 hours later he finished third in the Lightweight race after a photo–finish with Kawasaki-mounted Lawson and Mang.

In his first race after Daytona he was lucky to escape with a severe shaking when he crashed his Honda Superbike at over 100mph at Charlotte Motor Speedway when an oil filter came loose, the spillage coating his rear tyre.

A month later he crossed the Atlantic for that memorable European debut in the

Daytona 1980 and Freddie poses with his American-prepared 1,000cc Honda Superbike before his first race for the Japanese company.

Transatlantic Trophy races at Brands Hatch, Mallory Park and Oulton Park, in Britain. His performances during that Easter weekend brought him probably the most unique deal ever struck in motorcycle racing.

'While I was racing for Honda in the States I had a contract with Yamaha to race a 500 for them in Europe. I should think that was the first time a rider has had a contract with the two big Japanese companies at the same time."

Freddie continued, 'After the final Transatlantic race at Oulton Park we were invited to talk with Yamaha about the possibility of us getting involved for a few races.'

Yamaha gave him a production TZ500 to ride although he would have been happier with a works machine. It was sent to the States for Erv to prepare for Freddie to ride in the Belgian Grand Prix at Zolder. The whole of Europe was now waiting for his Grand Prix debut because

his opening sortie into Europe had proved so devastating at the Transatlantic Trophy.

After his two winning rides at Brands Hatch he went to the second round at the tiny Mallory Park circuit in Leicestershire, which could not be a greater contrast to the vast open spaces of Daytona.

Once again, to the amazement of the 50,000 British crowd, he matched the best in the world on his first visit to the tricky 1.35-mile circuit, finishing second in the first race behind Kenny Roberts and third in the second behind Roberts and Randy Mamola.

Then it was on to the 2.76-mile Oulton Park circuit in Cheshire for the final two rounds. Once again, despite using a reserve engine after seizing one the previous day at Mallory, he finished second to Roberts in the first race, but crashed without injury in the second while holding a comfortable lead.

'If I could go back I would do that one race a little different,' he confided. 'I had such a good lead I could have slowed up a little bit, but that was never my style. Now it is somewhat, because when I lead I try and pace myself. Bikes are so hard on tyres and equipment these days and you have to save them as much as you can.'

The crash got far more press coverage in Britain than it really merited, with certain reporters suggesting that 18-year-old 'Fast Freddie' was perhaps a little too inexperienced to stay in front of the likes of Roberts and Sheene on his first-ever visit to Europe.

'I wasn't going any faster than the previous race when I dragged down going into a left and fell, but of course the first thing that some people said was that I was not old enough to be going that fast. That's something I hate to hear and I hope that it's something that I will never say. People have the tendency to judge and criticize young people if they are going fast, saying obviously they don't know what they're doing because they're not old enough to have any experience. The same thing happened to me in my first year in the Grands Prix.'

Despite the crash the weekend was a fabulous success, with Freddie finishing second highest points scorer in the series behind Roberts. It had whetted the lad from Shreveport's appetite for European-style racing.

'The whole weekend was a dream and it will always be very special. It will always be special in my mind because of the feeling I had afterwards; the satisfaction of Erv after our problems at Daytona; the reception I got from the crowd; the jubilation of Mum and Dad. It was something I'd never experienced before.'

He had first ridden the TZ750 Yamaha in a club race at the Texas World Speedway, and

Long hair and ill-fitting leathers — Freddie in his new Honda colours at Daytona in 1980.

Early days with the American Honda Super-bike team — Freddie pushes the big four-stroke to the limit.

48

New man – new machine. Spencer on the two-stroke NS500 Honda leads Barry Sheene (Yamaha, no.7) and Kenny Roberts (Yamaha, no.3) during the 1982 Argentine Grand Prix.

Champion Sparking Plug's Jack Braken with Freddie before the disappointing Yamaha-mounted Grand Prix debut at Zolder in 1980.

More action from the 1982 Argentine Grand Prix – Kenny Roberts is on the limit (right) as he strives to get the better of Spencer (left) with Barry Sheene in hot pursuit.

after competing at Daytona was well tuned up for the Transatlantic Trophy races.

'It felt comfortable right from the beginning and bikes with a lot of power have never bothered me. My two greatest assets over the years have been my depth of perception and feel. I have the ability to judge distances and I've never used braking markers or any type of object to turn by or stop by. I always do it by feel and getting on to the 750 was not really an adjustment once I'd got used to the speed and acceleration. I really enjoyed it because it was very smooth and had a lot of power.

'Although it was my first time out of the States, being with Erv and the rest of the American team helped. I suppose I was a little bit naive because we turned up one day and were practising the next. I was excited about racing in front of so many people and I was so motivated when I got on the start line at Brands

Hatch that I was going out to win. I took to the circuit right away, the bike was running good and it just kind of happened. A sort of dream debut, I guess you could say.'

Four months later he was in Europe making his Grand Prix debut at Zolder, in Belgium, on the 500cc Yamaha with financial backing from German Mike Krauser. Being perfectly honest, Zolder, situated in the north central part of Belgium, is not noted for its hospitality and the fast, bumpy circuit was only used that once for a 500cc Grand Prix.

After tasting so much success at the Transatlantic Trophy both Freddie and the European fans were expecting great things. Both were very disappointed. The production Yamaha was not up to the task, while Belgium is a long way from America's hospitable deep South.

'Erv and I have talked about that Grand Prix

The Argentine classic again – this time it is the finishing order, with Kenny Roberts (Yamaha) leading from Barry Sheene (Yamaha) and Freddie Spencer (Honda).

Spencer (right) on the rostrum after the 1982 Argentine Grand Prix with winner Roberts (centre) and runner-up Sheene – at last Honda's plans were working out.

Belgian Grand Prix 1982 and Spencer (Honda) leads from Raymond Roche (Honda), Roberts (Yamaha) and Sheene (Yamaha).

Bronzed and relaxed despite set-backs in Austria and Spain, Freddie prepares for the Italian Grand Prix at Misano.

a lot of times since and even if we had the same machine we would have done things a lot different. Erv had put a lot of work into the bike and it could have been very competitive although at the time the production Yamahas were not considered that good.

'It was running very rich, which made it very peaky. Then on the start line I got baulked and my knee hit the gas tank and broke the fuel cock and I had to pull in after the first lap because gas was all over my tyres.'

Zolder was also very different to the lively Spencer household back in Shreveport. 'They locked us in the hotel we were staying in at nine o'clock at night and you could not get out', he recalled. 'The restaurant was closed and it was all so quiet and I was just not used to that. All my

life I'd gone to sleep with the TV on with Dad
working outside and it was just a lot different to
what I was used to, and of course I was a little
homesick. However, I knew when I went to the
grid to race and saw all the spectators and felt
the Grand Prix atmosphere that I wanted to
come back.'

Back home, despite winning on the Honda
Superbike at Elkhart Lake, Loudon and
Laguna Seca, it was Lawson riding the
Kawasaki that he had so nearly elected to use at
the beginning of the season, who took the AMA
Superbike title.

'We had a lot of engine failures, but I want to
give credit where credit is due to Dennis
McKay, who started up the race programme,
and Team Manager Steve McLaughlin, who

whipped it all into shape so very quickly. You
know he worked the people very hard, but it
worked and I think a lot of people were
surprised we were so competitive. It may have
hurt us later on in the year because the bikes
were so well tested we got too much power too
soon, and you can only push so hard.'

By the end of the 1980 season Freddie was
champing at the bit to go Grand Prix racing.
The problem was that Honda did not have a
competitive machine for him to use. Their
multi-million pound efforts with the four-
stroke NR500 were not proving at all
successful. To complicate matters, Yamaha
were desperately trying to persuade him to join
World Champion Kenny Roberts in their
Grand Prix team when he went to Japan to talk

The massed crowd at the 1982 Italian Grand Prix at Misano watches Marco Lucchinelli (Honda) lead Roberts (Yamaha) and Sheene (Yamaha) into the first corner with Spencer (Honda, no.22) in pursuit. Freddie came through to finish second to Franco Uncini (Suzuki, no.13).

about his future with the Honda hierachy.

He returned home with a three-year contract, plenty of promises and a plan to send Erv to Europe as the advance guard to plan his assault.

'My one-year contract was up at the end of 1980 and so once again I was faced with the decision of going to Europe with Yamaha or staying with Honda and racing in the States for at least another year,' he explained. 'They'd returned to the 500cc Grand Prix class with the NR500 four-stroke, but it was not competitive. Although they were not committed to building a two-stroke they indicated they would have something special by 1982. I wanted to stay with Honda because I liked the people and I knew we had a brilliant engine for the Superbike class. Also, the day before I was due to leave Japan, they told me they would take a CX500 and turn it through 90 degrss to make a vee-twin suitable for dirt-track racing – and that's how their dirt-track programme started. It was a way to keep me kind of pacified – well, not

really pacified, but interested.'

With Freddie staying at home they felt Erv should pave the way in Europe ready for the next season and so the very close partnership was split for a year. Erv went to work for former World Champion Barry Sheene in England.

Honda had dropped out of the World Championships in 1967. Before that, despite the considerable efforts of the late and great Mike Hailwood, they had never won the 500cc individual title. They returned to the fray 12 years later with the four-stroke NR500 to battle against the all-conquering two-strokes. Despite pouring millions of pounds into the project it was not a success, although it was Freddie who gave the machine its one and only victory before Honda realized that their future in the 500cc class rested with two-stroke power.

'During a break in the American season I went to Suzuka in Japan and rode the NR500 for a couple of laps and we decided to take it to Laguna Seca, in California, to race it.

'At first I was about six seconds outside the

lap record because I was trying to ride it like a normal motorcycle where you accelerate on the edge at around 13,000 revs. The four-stroke would rev to nearly 22,000 and so eventually I narrowed up the power band and brought the gears so close together that I was changing between 19,000 and 21,000 revs. I was shifting gears all the time, but you had to keep it in the power band if you were going to race it hard. Its great shortcomings were its weight and lack of torque.'

Despite these problems Freddie went out in the first heat and beat Kenny Roberts, which so pleased the Japanese they asked him to race the bike at the British Grand Prix, at Silverstone, a couple of weeks later.

For the first time the machine was on the second row of the grid when Freddie qualified in ninth place after pushing the very expensive four-stroke to its very limit. His biggest problem was push-starting the heavy machine into life and he spent hours practising on the runway at Silverstone, frightened he was going to be left on the line.

'If you didn't hit it just right it would skid the rear wheel and I had such a sore chest after that weekend banging the gas tank trying to get that thing started.'

He continued: 'In the middle of one of my practice sessions Carlo, quite an old Italian mechanic who went on to work for Marco Lucchinelli, came across after watching my efforts and said "I will show you". So this old guy took three or four steps and the bike started first time. I watched him and from that point on I didn't have a lot of trouble starting it.'

In the race he started in mid-field and to the delight of the British crowd he had raced his way through the pack into fifth place when the engine cried 'enough'. It was the closest the controversial and technically brilliant machine ever came to gaining a World Championship point.

'After getting started in mid-pack I'd worked up to fifth when it quit with the recurring problem of the valve springs getting weak and

Cossack-style cornering by Freddie on the NS500 Honda.

Flat on the tank, Barry Sheene (Yamaha) leads Spencer (Honda) during the 1982 Belgian Grand Prix.

After winning the 1982 Belgian Grand Prix, Freddie drops the Honda as he turns into the paddock. On the left Barry Sheene, runner-up, arrives on his Yamaha.

Recovering from his spill, Freddie Spencer salutes his first Grand Prix victory as Barry Sheene congratulates him.

eventually a piston hitting a valve. It was disappointing, but it was also certainly an experience to ride.'

Back home it was tough going, both with the new Honda dirt-tracker and the Superbike

A classic shot showing Freddie (Honda) leading Barry Sheene (Yamaha) during the 1982 Yugoslav Grand Prix.

road-racer. At Daytona his Superbike caught fire during a pit stop and he was lucky to be able to continue to finish third, while mechanical problems once again kept him out of the results in the 200-Miler. He eventually finished second to Lawson (Kawasaki) in the Superbike Championship and third in the Formula One.

Mechanical problems with the Honda meant he had to borrow an RG500 Suzuki for the 1981 Transatlantic Trophy races. It did not turn out to be a happy return to the series and just 12 months after taking the event by storm he finished just 10th highest points scorer and the American team were well beaten.

On the dirt the new Honda was also hitting plenty of problems, which in turn affected the road-racing programme. 'We had a lot of problems with the bike being so new,' he recalled. 'The bike was not competitive. It was water-cooled and it was heavy, but we were really into that programme trying to get it working and the Superbike effort suffered a little bit.'

Right in the middle of those troublesome days Japanese race personnel arrived at Honda America with a box. Making sure that only Freddie and Erv, who was over from England, were in the room, they opened it to reveal the new three-cylinder, two-stroke engine which was to form the basis of their challenge in the

The modern kness-out style of riding is well illustrated as Freddie cranks the Honda NS500 to the limit.

500cc World Championship. It was an important moment for everyone concerned.

'They unpacked this one engine and set it up there on the desk and Erv and I just looked. Erv said it looked more like a moto-cross engine, but then signed a contract with the factory. I was already under contract with a clause that said I could race both Superbike and dirt machines at home, depending on the competitiveness of the new two-stroke Grand Prix racer.

Freddie first tested the new NS500 machine in Japan in December 1981 and then went to Brazil with Italian World Champion Marco Lucchinelli, who had just joined Honda from Suzuki in a multi-thousand pound deal.

'The bike was nimble, but down on power a little bit, and we really were not sure how we stood until we raced it in a Grand Prix.'

That opening Grand Prix of the 1982 season illustrated just how sport can be unaffected by politics and even war. It was held on the outskirts of Buenos Aires, in Argentina, and just five days after the race round the 2.47-mile Autodromo Municipal de la Cuidad, Argentina invaded the Falkland Islands.

Freddie had never even heard of the Falklands when he arrived in bustling Buenos Aires. He had won the Superbike race at Daytona and, like the rest of the racing world, was anxious to discover how the new Honda two-stroke would perform against the best in the most competitive arena of motor sport.

It was pretty evident from the outset that Honda had got it right. He qualified in second place and in the 32-lap race was involved in a tremendous scrap with the works Yamahas of former World Champions Roberts and Sheene. He had to settle for third place at the finish, but with Lucchinelli fifth and Takazumi Katayama sixth on similar NS500 Hondas they were back in business in the 500cc class.

However, it was not going to be an easy passage and a broken crank kept him out of the results at the Austrian Salzburgring. The bad luck continued in Spain at the Jarama circuit. He had been fastest in practice and was leading the race when the three turned into a twin, thanks to a broken ignition lead.

The team stuck to their task and were rewarded with second place in the heat of the Italian Grand Prix on the Adriatic coast at Misano. It was Freddie's best Grand Prix result to date and he set a new lap record in his pursuit of Suzuki-mounted Franco Uncini, who went on to win the World Championship.

A crash in the pouring rain at Assen kept him out of the points at the Dutch TT, but just eight days later both Honda's comeback and Freddie's Grand Prix career took another giant step forward at the Belgian Grand Prix.

Action from the 1982 British Grand Prix at Silverstone as Spencer (Honda) leads Takazumi Katayama (Honda), Franco Uncini (Suzuki) and Kork Ballington (Kawasaki).

Smiling despite his problems, Freddie returns to the pits after crashing during the wet 1982 Dutch TT.

The 4.332-mile Spa-Francorchamps circuit weaves its way through a tree-lined valley high in the Ardennes and is one of the classic Grand Prix venues. Not only was it the perfect setting for the Belgian Grand Prix, but it was also a perfect day for an American victory. July 4 is American Independence Day, and Freddie celebrated it by winning his first Grand Prix and giving Honda their first victory in the 500cc class for the 15 years, since Hailwood had won the Canadian Grand Prix. Roberts had led, but faded with tyre problems and 20-year-old Freddie raced into the lead, never to be headed.

It was the greatest day of his racing life to date, and after crossing the line he slowed to walking pace. Then, while making an acute turn back to the pits the excitement was too much and he fell from his Honda, slumping into an undignified heap before being mobbed by celebrating well-wishers.

Just two months later he was back on the Grand Prix victory rostrum after a start-to-finish win in the San Marino Grand Prix in the scorching heat of Mugello.

The final Grand Prix of the season was at Hockenheim, in West Germany, and Freddie was only 4 points adrift of New Zealander Graeme Crosby, who lay second in the championlship table riding in Giacomo Agostini's Marlboro Yamaha team. Freddie's chances of finishing runner-up in the championship looked almost certain when Crosby crashed on the 15th lap. Freddie was leading at the time and appeared to be heading for a comfortable victory when he started to slow two laps from the finish with ignition problems.

As he raced into the stadium on the last lap the 100,000 paying customers were on their feet. Randy Mamola and World Champion Uncini had closed right up on him as he prepared to peel off into the tight left-hander just 500 yards from the finish. His pit signals had warned him of the impending danger but he had not realized they were so close, and did not even look behind as he braked. Mamola managed to dive underneath him, but Uncini was committed and could not get through the gap. He clipped the back wheel of the Honda and both went down. Uncini was unhurt, but Freddie was soon on his way to hospital with concussion, a broken collarbone and, worse still, only third place in the World Championship.

The next time he raced a bike was at Daytona in March 1983. He won the Superbike race, but retired in the '200' with transmission problems. He was ready for the opening Grand Prix of the year at Kyalami, in South Africa. Twelve races and seven months later he was to be Champion of the World.

60

Victory in sight — Spencer on the NS500 Honda heads for his second Grand Prix victory in the San Marino Grand Prix at Mugello in 1982.

On the rostrum at Mugello, Freddie (centre) celebrates with runner-up Randy Mamola (left) and third-placed Graeme Crosby who has doubled up on the sponsors' head-gear.

Freddie wheelies the NS500 Honda at the German Grand Prix at Hockenheim in 1982. A collision near the end cost him second place in the 500cc World Championship. In the paddock, below, he demonstrates a similar feat on the Honda scooter he used as a paddock runabout.

A private man

The champion off track

A Grand Prix motorcycle racing paddock is very similar to a small town community. The obvious difference is that every Sunday evening it packs up to move on to another venue, which will be home for four or five days during practice and racing at the next Grand Prix.

Despite these constant upheavals it is a tight-knit community. At the top you have the massive works teams with their motorhomes, support vehicles and tented encampments, while at the other end of the scale there are riders living out of vans and just about scraping an existence to go racing.

The very nature of the sport, with its speed, glamour and the constant reminder of danger, breeds outgoing characters who have never been slow to voice their opinions. Recent World 500cc Champions such as Barry Sheene, Italian Marco Lucchinelli and Kenny Roberts have never been long out of the headlines with their exploits, both on and more often off the tracks. The sport thrived on these characters, who were not only brilliant and brave motorcycle racers, but enjoyed life and their success to the full.

Freddie then arrives on the scene. The ice-cool shy professional with deep religious beliefs. Non-smoking and almost teetotal, who between practice sessions could be found in his massive motorhome, with Louisiana number-plates, drinking a can of his favourite cola and watching basketball videos from home. Very rarely was he seen walking through the paddock or passing the time of day in idle chat. Girlfriend Sarie flew in to watch him race as often as her college and beauty queen commitments would allow, while he flew home, often on Concorde, as often as he could between races to be with his family and friends.

Four years and three World Championships later his routine has not changed that much, although the pressures, both mental and physical, of chasing the 250 and 500 'double' and satisfying the needs of Rothmans, the Honda team's sponsors, have meant even less spare time for somebody who takes racing very seriously.

During his 'double' year the critics have called him aloof and a loner. Freddie respects these critics and their opinions. He does not pretend that he does not take racing very seriously, while also feeling a little ill at ease being the constant centre of attention.

'I don't scowl or anything, but I've never been one who's too comfortable around large crowds of people,' he revealed. 'Of course I appreciate fans, and I don't resent them in any way. They are a vital part of racing, but I just don't feel real comfortable.'

Racing is a dangerous game, with massive rewards for the very successful, and perhaps it is a little unfair to label somebody aloof because they are constantly seeking ways to improve their skills.

'At the race-track I'm serious. It's my job, and I'm not there to have fun. I have to

concentrate on what I'm doing and I'm always trying to perfect my craft. In the last couple of years I've been the only Honda factory rider and so the four-cylinder project was all basically mine and that also carries a lot of responsibility with Michelin. I have done all the tyre testing and have put all my efforts into it.'

Back home and among family and friends and in familiar surroundings he's a very different character. Fiancée Sarie, a former Miss Louisiana, is his constant companion. They met through friends who felt they could make the ideal match and from that day the friends' judgment has never been doubted. His family and religious upbringing have made him appreciate home life, which is even more welcome after spending a long time away in Europe.

'Away from the race-track and especially at home I'm far more outgoing and at ease,' explained Freddie, who sponsors a local softball team while running his own dirt-track team. 'I go to movies. I love playing softball, I play basketball, I get knocked around a bit, and I have a lot of fun. I give my heart and soul when I'm out there racing and so I must get away to get my perspective back and get a fresh outlook so that when the next season rolls around I will be ready to go again.'

Freddie makes a comment after inspecting the front tyre of his Honda at the 1984 Dutch TT.

Between practice sessions Freddie relaxes with his paddock transport.

Rivals – but friends. Freddie (right) back-to-back with fellow American Eddie Lawson.

He is also turning his success on the track into business ventures which he follows very closely as President of Freddie Spencer and Companies Inc. There is a Honda dealership in Shreveport, and the company is involved in investment and property dealings further afield.

'I enjoy being involved with the company and the office. We do a lot of things together and I've just invested in a project which is only a mile away from the Texas World Speedway. Really that's a dream to think I'd be down there investing money in something so close to where I got started in racing and gained my experience.'

Without a shadow of doubt the most publicized aspect of Freddie's life is his religion. Somehow the image of Grand Prix motorcycling does not lend itself to religious

beliefs. For Freddie a life without his belief in God is quite unthinkable, although nothing makes him more angry than being called a born-again Christian or a Mormon.

'Basically I'm a baptist and not a Mormon, and I've never been to Utah,' he explained. 'I went to a Christian school and that had a great deal of influence. Myself and my friends go to church and it's something very personal. It gets talked about a lot, but it gives me inner confidence and inner strength; something to believe in, and I think that's the most important thing in life.'

He continued, 'I've seen so many young kids and so many people in America who don't have anything to believe in and you can see this because they just wonder. They don't believe in anything or in themselves and I think that what

Like most star riders Freddie prefers to live in a motorhome in the paddock rather than a hotel. Here he poses with the vehicle he used in 1982.

Freddie holds an informal press conference in his motorhome after yet another win.

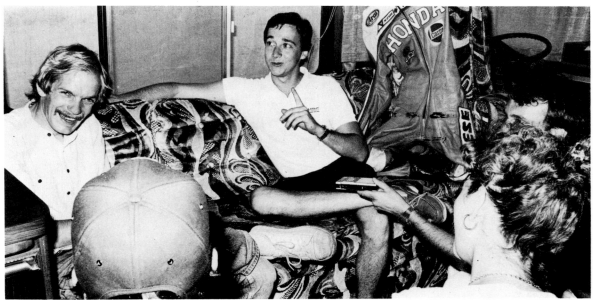

Business man Freddie Spencer about to jet back to his Shreveport home from Europe. How many would guess this man is the world's top motorcycle racer?

Like many successful Americans Freddie enjoys a round of golf. Here he gets into the swing of things on a Dutch course.

I believe in gives me the strength to know what I can accomplish; that I have the ability to accomplish something and to point me in the right direction. I'm a firm believer in the old saying that God helps those who help themselves and I just don't believe it comes easy. It doesn't. Nothing worthwhile comes easy.'

That total belief, coupled with his parents' massive influence, shaped his future and gave him that confidence and belief in his own ability.

69

Waiting for the start . . . . at Hockenheim in 1983.

'Dad gave me the control to build-up my own self-confidence and to implement my own self-discipline, and racing is responsible for a lot of that. It has helped me to grow up and to understand, not only what I've sacrificed, but to appreciate what sacrifices other people have made and to appreciate their abilities. It goes back to not being stifled and told what to do. A lot of things were left up to me to make my own decisions at an early age.'

One of the decisions Freddie took many years ago was that he would never race while injured. While many riders will take pain-killing injections and have bones pinned to enable them to race as soon as possible after accidents he will only ride again after his injuries have healed. Critics have suggested that his insistence on not riding while injured probably cost him the 1984 World Title. Certainly pain-killing injections may have allowed him to race with his injured feet, while pinning may have enabled him to compete a couple of weeks after breaking his collarbone. That's not Freddie's style and never will be.

'I'm not the type who rides injured or wants to ride injured. I've been racing a very long time, and I've seen people – and you can see them in other sports too – who go out and abuse their body and they are not around very long. One of the greatest running backs of all time in American Football, Earl Campbell, would run with pulled hamstrings, with a twisted ankle and other injuries. He probably would have been THE greatest if he had given himself time to heal.

'The worst thing that could happen to me would be to be mentally and emotionally able to race, but not have the physical tools to do it. Without those you cannot be 100 per cent and it can happen so easily. Of course, some people will criticize me for it, while others understand. I do what I think is right, and there's a lot more to life than racing. I think that a lot of people don't look ahead, and that's what I've always tried to do.'

So what does the future hold for somebody who has already achieved all the goals that Grand Prix motorcycle racing can offer? Will his appetite be satisfied by chasing his third world 500cc title, or will be seek pastures new?

'You know, I love racing and it's been a very big part of my life and it's given me so much,' he explained. 'You can plan for retiring as much as you like, but its something that just comes. I'm not sure when that will be for me, although when I do decide to quit that will be the end of racing for me.

'I'm just going to take one year at a time, and right now the number-one priority will be to win the 500cc title once again. I've had the

opportunity to race a car in the US, but I will just have to wait and see.'

When he does decide to seek fresh pastures the Grand Prix paddock will never be quite the same without him. He is an amazing combination of controlled aggression and purpose, offset by a basic shyness of fuss and publicity, the like of which have never been seen in Grand Prix racing before.

An American magazine summed him up perfectly when they said: 'His courteousness and Southern gentility is a throwback to a different era, from long before World Championship Grand Prix motorcycle racing started in 1949.'

Trackside conference between Spencer and technical adviser Erv Kanemoto

A kiss on the helmet from fiancée Sarie as Freddie prepares for battle.

Chapter of accidents

1984, season of setbacks

News of a crash spreads through a Grand Prix paddock like a fire. News of a crash involving the World Champion spreads even quicker – and barely had Freddie hit the Kyalami tarmac with a fearful bump than the whole paddock knew. Thirty minutes later news bulletins around the world were reporting his crash but with the World Champion barely limping through the paddock nobody took too much notice or was that concerned. After all, the 1984 South African Grand Prix was still two days away, and he was sure to be fit to start the defence of his title.

Back in his hotel room on the outskirts of Johannesburg, Freddie was beginning to hurt, and even walking across the room to reach the 'phone was starting to prove a problem. By the evening he was in real pain and the doctor was called. He diagnosed torn ligaments in the right ankle and deep bruising on the left foot. The next time Freddie used wheels for propulsion was not sitting astride the NSR V4 Honda on the starting grid, but sitting in a wheelchair pushed by Erv as they scurried through Jan Smuts airport on the Saturday night with his ankle in plaster . . .

'All I could do was sit and watch Eddie Lawson win the race on the television in my hotel room, which was all pretty frustrating,' he revealed as he boarded the London-bound plane in rather different circumstances to his arrival in South Africa just six days earlier.

It was a bad blow for the Champion and his confidence, especially as the crash had happened in rather frightening circumstances when the carbon-fibre rear wheel of his machine just collapsed as he swung through the Esses in the first official practice session.

'As I went into the corner the front end just went light and the back collapsed and the next thing I knew I was sliding into the straw bales.'

It had all looked so different when he arrived in the sunshine to start practising. Two weeks earlier, at Daytona, he had comfortably won the Superbike race and, more important, gave a very impressive debut to the new four-cylinder NSR500 Honda in the 200-Miler. He finished second to Kenny Roberts, riding the very fast 680cc Yamaha, after the Honda slowed with a split exhaust pipe while battling for the lead.

However, that Daytona result did not reflect the problems he was going to experience with the new machine, which ultimately resulted in the loss of his cherished championship crown. At first all seemed well. Indeed, at the second Grand Prix of the season, at Misano, in Italy, Freddie had recovered well from the South African accident and cruised to victory on the new machine with Lawson second nearly 20 seconds adrift. While it was a great result, there were problems just around the corner.

'Of all the tracks we used in the championship, Misano was the best for the V4,' he revealed. 'I won comfortably and everything went so well we were totally unprepared for the troubles we would have later in the season. We

Thumbs up from Freddie Spencer during winter testing of the all new four-cylinder NSR500 Honda at Surfers Paradise, Australia, in December 1983 but the unorthodox machine proved a disappointment.

found out later that the machine lacked torque, but at Misano you run really close gearbox ratios and the engine is always revving hard and so it was no problem.'

He did not even make it to the next round of the Championship in Spain. Instead, he heard the result sitting at home in Shreveport with his feet up talking to BBC Radio Two, who were broadcasting live from the circuit. It did not make good listening, because Lawson was in great form and won the race. With three rounds gone the seemingly comfortable defence of his title was turning into a nightmare – he was already 27 points down.

His enforced absence from Jarama was caused by a crash in the fifth leg of the Transatlantic Trophy, at Donington Park. He was leading comfortably when he dumped the NSR at Redgate Corner, and once again it was his feet that took the brunt. For the previous two days Freddie and the rest of the Americans had thrilled millions of British television viewers with a magnificent display of riding that prompted former World Champion Barry Sheene to say, Freddie was the greatest rider he had ever seen. Happily, Barry did not change his opinion after the incident at Redgate on Easter Monday afternoon.

Freddie: 'This time the crash was partly my fault. The NSR has really different handling

First race on the new NSR500 four-cylinder was at Daytona in March 1984. Here Freddie Spencer pursues Kenny Roberts on the far more powerful 680cc Yamaha.

characteristics from the NS500 and they really showed up at Donington and, quite frankly, just caught me out. Redgate Corner is one that you accelerate really hard all the way through and the crash happened because the front-end of the bike turned in. On the NS500, when this begins to happen, you simply have to give it more throttle so that it picks up the front wheel and straightens itself out. The V4 is very different because of the totally changed weight distribution.

'With the fuel tank under the engine the weight of the fuel is transferred forward under braking and tends to push the front wheel. Therefore if the bike does turn in you can't compensate with a burst of throttle. You have to use some muscle and actually pick the bike up. I used too much muscle, too quickly, and the bike reacted faster than I thought. It got some grip and pitched me over the high side.'

Injuries heal, and although he returned for the fourth round of the championship at the very fast Salzburgring, in Austria, he left there a very worried man after finishing second to Lawson in controversial circumstances.

'We realized after Austria that the NSR500, although potentially a superb machine, needed far more development time. My fastest lap in practice was 1.2 seconds slower than I'd achieved the year before on the three-cylinder

Disaster in South Africa. Marshals run to the aid of Spencer who ended up amid the straw-bales after the new carbon-fibre rear wheel of the NSR500 Honda broke during practice.

NS500. There was no way we were going to win, and just had to make the most of it. I did get second, but actually felt lucky to get the 12 points.'

Indeed, on the slowing-up lap many of the 80,000 Austrian crowd jammed on the grass banks that make vast natural grandstands around the picturesque circuit, booed both Freddie and his new team-mate Randy Mamola. He had slowed dramatically on the last lap on his NS500, allowing Spencer to take over second place and the crowd did not like it.

The official programme for the Austrian Grand Prix that year had a picture of Freddie on the cover riding the NS500 three-cylinder

Honda and just seven days later he was back on his old trusty steed for the German Grand Prix, at the new Nürburgring circuit in the Eifel mountains.

During the first official practice session on the Friday morning round the new 2.82-mile course, which had cost nearly £25 million to build, it was painfully obvious to Freddie and the team that the NSR V4 was not ready to take on the might of Lawson and his Marlboro Yamaha. At the end of the day he was only ninth fastest and it was decision time. Swallowing their pride, Honda sent mechanic Stuart Shenton to their race headquarters in Belgium and he returned in the early hours of the

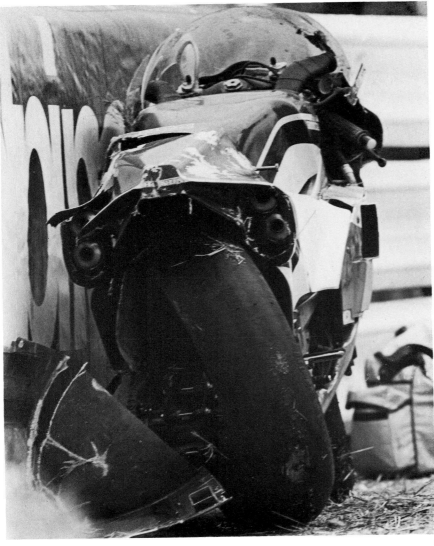

The collapsed rear wheel of Spencer's NSR500 Honda at the South African Grand Prix. The incident put him out of the race with an ankle injury.

Winning again! Freddie Spencer wheelies with joy as he wins the Italian Grand Prix at Misano. His first success on the NSR500, it proved to be a false dawn.

morning with the NS500 that had been ridden by Marco Lucchinelli the previous year.

By the end of the day Freddie had qualified in pole position and in the 30-lap race he stormed away from the opposition, led by Lawson. It was a morale-boosting victory, although Freddie was disappointed it was on the old machine.

'Obviously it was great to win the race, but now we were a little worried about the development pace of the new V4,' he admitted. 'During practice at the Nürburgring we could see some improvement, but it wasn't coming quick enough, and so I had to race the triple.'

However, the hard work on the new machine was slowly paying dividends. After victories on

the V4 at the next two Grands Prix Freddie was only 17 points adrift of Lawson, and still in with a chance.

The fight back had started at the French Grand Prix at the 3.61-mile Paul Ricard circuit in the delightful Provence region near the Mediterranean coast. Strangely, the race was held on a Monday in order not to clash with the final of the French Open Tennis Championship the previous day. After qualifying in pole position Freddie sat with fiancèe Sarie in the press box and watched Ivan Lendl beat John McEnroe on the television. The next day he performed a similar feat against Eddie Lawson.

'At Paul Ricard our fears about the V4 were

Close up of the Freddie Spencer style on the NSR500 — but he crashed soon after while competing in the Transatlantic Trophy series at Donington Park and suffered injuries that kept him out of the Spanish Grand Prix.

Freddie was back in action for the fourth classic of the year – the Austrian Grand Prix. Here (left) he leads Sheene (Yamaha, no.7) and Lawson (Yamaha, no.4) off the line; Mamola has already gone. Lawson won the race with Spencer second.

somewhat allayed because it was an ideal track for the machine's power characteristics, with long straights and fast corners. I won quite comfortably and all-in-all it was a good race for us because we were starting to see some progress, and there was obviously a lot more potential there.'

Just six days later the team were positively glowing in the Yugoslavian humidity when Freddie took the lead on the third lap and raced away from his pursuers. Equally important, his Honda team-mates Mamola and Frenchman Raymond Roche pushed Lawson down into fourth place where he claimed just 8 World Championship points after suffering tyre problems that slewed him sideways every time he poured on the power.

You do not win 15 world titles without learning a great deal about how the sport works, and so when Marlboro Yamaha team boss Giacomo Agostini spotted a flaw in Honda strategy at the Dutch TT, the eighth round of the World Championship, he exploited it to the full.

It was that decision by Agostini that did so much to snatch the World Championship out of Freddie's grasp.

Freddie practised on the V4 before the massive Dutch crowds, but those old problems showed up round the demanding Circuit van Drenthe, which had been reduced in length to 3.812 miles. At the end of timed practice he found himself down in fifth qualifying position. Freddie decided to go out and try the old three-

80

That's the way to do it – Spencer won the Belgian Grand Prix at Spa-Francorchamps on the three-cylinder NS500 Honda in a season that was more often disastrous than successful. As it turned out, Spa was his last race of the 1984 season.

Close tussle on the La Source hairpin at Spa, with Raymond Roche (Honda, no.11) running wide, and Mamola, Spencer and Haslam coming through on the inside.

Ron Haslam (Honda) leads at the start of the German Grand Prix at the new Nürburgring but Spencer (Honda, no.1) back on the NS500 three-cylinder, came through to win.

By the German Grand Prix it was obvious that Eddie Lawson (left) who had taken over from Kenny Roberts as leader of the Yamaha team, was the man most likely to take Spencer's world crown.

Knee skimming the ground on the far side, Freddie Spencer corners the NSR500 four-cylinder during his winning ride at the French Grand Prix.

cylinder machine in the unofficial session before the race, but Agostini had done his homework and stepped in.

Waving a set of the supplementary regulations, he pointed out that Freddie had not practised on the three-cylinder during the timed sessions and so could not use it in the race. There were a few grey areas about the validity of the regulations, but Honda could not risk disqualification and so out came the V4 on to the grid.

'On the morning of the race we made some carburation changes which resulted in a big improvement and I actually felt pretty confident,' he recalled. 'By the second lap I was in the lead when suddenly a plug lead came off and, ironically, the bike became a three-cylinder. I got back to the pits and the crew replaced it, but after another 500 metres it came off again and I was out of the running.'

While Lawson uncharacteristically sulked in his motorhome after only finishing third behind Mamola and Roche, Freddie admitted to the assembled press that his World Championship was slipping away.

'In many ways I felt the championship result was now out of our hands,' he said. 'We just have to hope that Lawson will have trouble.'

Just eight days later his predictions had a slightly hollow ring when he won the Belgian Grand Prix at Spa-Francorchamps. He had ridden both the three and four-cylinder machines in practice, but stuck to the three for the race and cruised to victory. Just as important, Lawson was again beset with tyre troubles and could only manage fourth place behind Mamola and Roche. The gap was down to 20 points and Freddie still had a chance – until a warm Californian afternoon two weeks later, when his year came to an abrupt end.

A record 85,000 crowd had assembled to see Kenny Roberts, in what he told us was his last road-racing appearance, take on Freddie at Laguna Seca. Unfortunately, they went home disappointed because Freddie did not even make the line.

Spencer crosses the line at the Circuit Paul Ricard to win the 1984 French Grand Prix – a success that put him back into contention for the World Championship.

'I crashed during practice, re-breaking the collarbone that I'd broken at Hockenheim in 1982,' he explained. 'It took six weeks to mend and so I missed the British and Swedish races and could do nothing as Eddie had won the Championship by the time I was fit to race. I could have made the final Grand Prix at Mugello, in Italy, but the bikes had already been sent back to Japan.'

At the beginning of the Grand Prix season just five incident-packed months earlier, Freddie had been the biggest favourite to retain his title for over a decade.

He had been the youngest rider ever to win the 500cc crown, and with Honda's massive backing he looked odds-on for further honours. Motorcycle racing at any level has a great habit of wrecking any predictions, and sitting back in Shreveport, unable to lift a finger to prevent Lawson stealing his crown, made him very determined.

'Of course the year was a bit of a disaster for me, but it wasn't all bad. I proved to myself that I was as fast a rider as I ever had been, which partly made up for the disappointment of losing the Championship. I can go into 1985 with a lot of confidence. In fact, I've put the bad stuff about 1984 totally out of my mind and I'm concentrating on the good points. I'm as confident about racing as I ever was, and I'll guarantee right now that 1985 is going to be a different story for Freddie Spencer and Honda.'

Even Freddie, after making that brave prediction in September of that year, could not have realized in his wildest dreams that next year he would be chasing and winning not one world title – but two!

The Double

250 and 500 – a world record

From the moment he screamed past the chequered flag after 100 trouble-free miles round the Daytona speed bowl on his RS250R Honda to win the Lightweight race at the 1985 Florida classic, Freddie knew that the 'double' was on.

Throughout the winter he'd been thinking very hard about tackling both the 250 and 500cc world titles the next season. What better way to make up for the disappointments of the previous season, and what better way to introduce tobacco giants Rothmans into the sport just after they'd signed a sponsorship deal with the Honda team? All that was really needed to push Freddie into a final decision was proof that the 250 Honda was competitive and that the changes promised by Honda on the NSR500 had been carried out.

A week in March on the Florida coastline at Daytona was proof enough, and the 'double' that had even eluded the great Mike Hailwood and Kenny Roberts was on.

'I like goals and I need challenges, and after last season it was something I needed to get back into and something to really work hard for,' he explained. 'We talked about it in 1984 when Honda brought out their 250cc production racer and as the year went on we talked about it more and more. I rode the 250 for the first time at Suzuka in early September and it wasn't a bad little machine. I tested it again in Australia, and then raced it for the first time at Daytona, together with the new NSR500, and I knew from that moment that, the 'double' was possible.'

Although the opposition was not of the highest quality at Daytona he won the 100-miler on the Friday afternoon, riding the new NSR – with the fuel tank conventionally mounted above the engine – first time out, and then dominated the Lightweight race the next morning. The first Grand Prix of the season, in South Africa, was just two weeks away and as an American journalist at Daytona explained: 'That would be a completely new ball game after Daytona.'

The heat, altitude and the determination of Lawson, fired up by criticism that he was a lucky World Champion, certainly made it a very different ball game for the Rothmans Honda team. However, this time Freddie did not leave the airport in a wheelchair, but with trophies from his first win in the 250cc class and a second place in the 500cc race after a fiercely-contested encounter with Lawson. It gave him a graphic indication of the size of the task he had embarked on – he knew it was going to be tough.

The 250cc Grand Prix regulars who had provided such close racing for the past three years were determined to give Freddie a tough time. Former World Champions Toni Mang, from West Germany, riding the Marlboro Honda and Venezuelan Carlos Lavado, on the works Yamaha, pushed him hard after Freddie had led into the first bend in the scorching heat.

First win of the incredible double – Freddie leads the field at the start of the 250cc South African Grand Prix.

Both Mang, who was mad with Honda because he did not have a works machine similar to Spencer's, and Lavado, led until Freddie pulled away for a comfortable 7-second victory to record Honda's first win in the 250cc class since 1967.

Mang, who had won both the 250 and 350cc world titles for Kawasaki, was impressed. 'Although I was faster in the corners than Freddie, he would just wait and pass me on the straight,' he explained. 'Spencer on the new bike is a pretty formidable proposition.' Lavado felt that Freddie would not find it so easy when the Grand Prix circus arrived back in Europe. 'The circuit was ideally suited to Freddie and his new Honda, but I hope he does not think it will be so easy all the time,' he said. 'It will be different at the tighter, more demanding European circuits.'

A quick shower and a change of leathers after

rushing from the victory rostrum and it was back to the grid to start 30 energy-sapping laps in the 500cc race. Freddie took the lead from Ron Haslam on the first lap, but Lawson was soon on his tail and the pair pulled away to fight their own magnificent duel in the sun.

On lap 8 Lawson took the lead, and despite both riders having problems with tyres and back-markers Freddie could do nothing to stop him. He was never close enough to mount a serious challenge, although he had set a new lap record in the early stages. Obviously the earlier race and the heat and altitude had taken their toll.

'Of course I'm disappointed at not winning the 500, but we could not have picked a harder start to the 'double' than at Kyalami in the heat and altitude,' he explained at the airport. 'It was tough, but the new 250 went very well. We are having a few handling problems with the 500,

Fifteen times World Champion Giacomo Agostini congratulates Freddie after his 250cc South African win.

Reigning champion Eddie Lawson (Yamaha) leads the 500cc race in South Africa with Freddie in hot pursuit — but Lawson held on to win.

On his way – a splendid Don Morley shot of Freddie in action on the four-cylinder 500cc Honda NSR-500 at Spa-Francorchamps during the Belgian Grand Prix. At this eighth round of the World series, he scored a clear victory in both 250cc and 500cc races.

Freddie (left) talks to compatriot Randy Mamola before the start of the Spanish Grand Prix.

which we will sort out. After all, this time last year I was leaving here in a wheelchair.'

Over a month elapsed before the second round of the championship in Spain, but Freddie was busy tyre testing at Rijeka, in Yugoslavia. He did not race in the Transatlantic Trophy series in Britain, following his crash the previous year.

He was not happy with the handling of the NSR500, but after also practising on the three-cylinder NS500 for the Spanish Grand Prix he stuck to the four-cylinder machine. This turned out to be the correct choice, although it was an incident-packed event.

Freddie crashed during untimed practice in the morning, hurting his thumb. Then the start of the 37-lap race was delayed half an hour by heavy rain, and when the riders were flagged away former World Champion Franco Uncini slid off his Suzuki just 10 yards after the start of the warm-up lap.

Once underway Freddie took the lead from Haslam on the sixth lap when he dived under the British star at the right-hander at the end of the start and finish straight and powered away from Lawson, who made no excuses after finishing 14 seconds down in second place.

'I had no real problems, but I was just not quick, enough to catch Freddie today,' he admitted. Freddie looked set for the 'double'

when he was leading the 250cc just an hour later when disaster struck, and he was lucky to limp home in ninth place.

'I was leading by 7 seconds when a big hole blew in my exhaust, and once I heard that dreaded noise I knew exactly what had happened because I'd had the same problem with the 500 at Daytona the previous year. I was really enjoying the race up 'til then, but after that all I could do was count the riders going past me and just hope I could stay in the points.'

Stay in the points he did, but dropped to fourth place in the 250cc championship table, 6 points behind the leader Lavado. In the 500cc class he shared the lead with Lawson, but both were in for a shock two weeks later in the pouring rain at Hockenheim, in West Germany.

Since Kenny Roberts led the way 11 years ago, American riders have enjoyed enormous success in the Grands Prix, and incredibly for nearly three years had won every 500cc Grand Prix. Japanese ace Takazumi Katayama was the last non-American to stand on the winner's rostrum when he won the Swedish Grand Prix in 1982 – that was until Frenchman Christian Sarron arrived at Hockenheim on May 19, 1985.

In appalling conditions Sarron, then the reigning 250cc World Champion, was

Venezuelan Carlos Lavado (Yamaha) leads but Freddie is shadowing him and came through to win the 250cc class of the Italian Grand Prix at Mugello — a win that put him at the top of both the 250cc and 500cc World Championship tables.

Paddock racer — Freddie with the Honda scooter he used for between races transport in 1985.

unbeatable on the puddle-ridden, tree-lined circuit on his Gauloises-sponsored Sonauto Yamaha. He rode from 10th place to snatch the lead from Freddie just eight laps from the finish of the 19-lap race.

'Christian rode a brilliant race and deserved to win. My rear tyre began to spin in the wet and there was nothing I could do to catch him. However, my pit signals told me that Eddie was down in fourth place and so I knew if I could keep Haslam out of second place I would head the championship by four points.'

That is exactly what happened, and the earlier 250cc race was almost a carbon copy with West German Martin Wimmer bringing the massive home crowd to their feet by leading Freddie over the line by over 11 seconds. He moved into the lead in the championship table, just four points in front of Freddie, who was third after previous leader Lavado had crashed in the race. The 'double machine' was gaining momentum and it received a massive boost at the next two Grands Prix in Italy and Austria.

Freddie was slowly getting used to the pressures, both mental and physical, of practising and riding in two classes. Some people, and certain frustrated journalists who

250 dice in Austria – left, Freddie (Honda, no.19) leads challenger Toni Mang (Honda, no.5) and, right, saluting the crowd on their lap of honour.

found his time was very limited for interviews, felt he was becoming too much a loner, snatching a rest in his motorhome between practice sessions and races. Visits to the motorhome were strictly but fairly supervised by his able lieutenant Iain 'Mac' Mackay. It was a tough and demanding time for the whole team.

'I'm not a person to waste time, and I don't take my abilitiy to win or my ability to test and solve problems for granted,' Freddie explained to a journalist who ask why he was never seen strolling round the paddock. 'Of course, this year has been doubly difficult. The 500 is a new machine, which makes it very difficult. We had so many tyres I had to test and so many gear ratios and engine combinations to choose from.

I would go out on the 250 and check the tyres and the suspension on two different machines and then get off them and do exactly the same on the 500s. Afterwards, I would have to try and separate the two in my mind because there was not often a gap between 250 and 500 practice. I would spend the next hour with Erv going over the problems and then start all over again. The qualifying was usually back-to-back, and so I'd have to store the information about the 250s and then clear my mind and get on a 500 and then afterwards remember all the details about both.

'So the mental aspect was the most difficult thing of the season. Fortunately, physically I was really prepared for I knew it was going to be difficult. After last season I worked very hard

Competing in both World Championships put quite a strain on Freddie at each 1985 Grand Prix. Rothmans girls protect him from the sun and the crowd on the grid at Spa, as well as advertising their wares as the Honda team's sponsors.

Start-line action as Lawson (Yamaha, no.1) gets away ahead of Spencer in the Yugolslav Grand Prix. Lawson went on to win.

because the main thing was to recover very fast, physically. The recovery time after getting off the 500 onto the 250 or vice versa is very short. Because I was very fit I didn't have to worry about getting tired. If you are tired that drains you mentally because you have to concentrate harder. If you get mentally tired when you are physically strong you can usually catch and correct a mistake.'

Freddie had no reason to correct any mistakes at the fourth round of the championship at the picturesque Mugello circuit, nestling in the Tuscan hills above Florence, in Italy.

He became the first rider since the late Finnish star Jarno Saarinen, 12 years earlier, to win both a 250 and 500 Grand Prix in the same afternoon. Despite tyre problems he cruised away from Lawson in the 27-lap 500 race to open up a 7-point lead in the championship.

Just half an hour later he was involved in a tremendous 250cc race in which he fought his

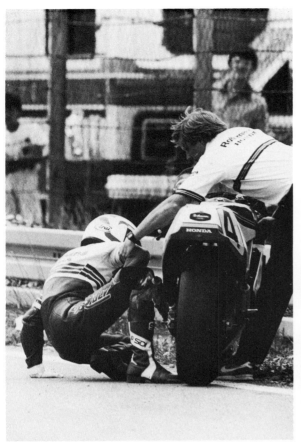

Dramatic moment at the end of the 500cc Yugoslav Grand Prix as Freddie collapses from his Honda. He had struck his right knee on a straw-bale early in the race and had ridden on in agony to finish second. The pictures show him falling from his machine, looking dazed after his helmet had been removed and being carried to the first-aid room.

Less than two weeks after his Yugoslavian accident, Freddie heads for victory in the 250cc Dutch TT.

way through the field to overtake Lavado five laps from the finish. For the first time he led both World Championships, and that was a situation that never changed.

He repeated the 'double dose' just a week later at the Austrian Salzburging, although it was a very, very close thing – a matter of just three-hundredths of a second!

In the 25-lap 250cc race he saw off the challenge of Mang and Italian Fausto Ricci riding a Rothmans Honda. The 500cc race was very different, especially as it was stopped in the middle when the rain began to fall.

Freddie was leading at the time, with Lawson second. The second leg was won by Lawson, but agonizingly for the World Champion, when the times for the two races were added together

Freddie stole the verdict and the 15 World Championship points by just those three-hundredths of a second. Lawson was bitterly disappointed and went to the sixth round in Yugoslavia 10 points down.

That bitter disappointment turned to joy in the heat of the 32-lap race round the Autodromo at Rijeka. Lawson was determined to pull back the lead, and at the finish Freddie collapsed from his machine. He was rushed to the medical centre. As Lawson waved to the crowds at the victory ceremony, less than 100 yards away behind the grandstand, Freddie was having his leg and thigh X-rayed by Italian Dr Claudio Costa, who runs the Grand Prix mobile medical centre. He had clouted a straw-bale with his knee early in the race while chasing

96

Perfectly poised . . . . Freddie on the 500cc Honda practising for the Dutch TT.

Lawson and had collapsed in agony at the finish.

'I honestly did not think I could finish the race because I was in so much pain, and I thought I'd broken something,' he explained before flying straight back to Shreveport for treatment. 'I was lucky to finish second because on many occasions I thought I was going to pass out, but somehow I managed to stay on.'

Before all the drama he had been a comfortable winner of the 250cc race, and with the X-rays showing no breaks, he was declared fit for the Dutch TT at Assen, just 13 days later.

The flat and featureless Dutch landscape is at its most depressing when the rain pours down, and at Assen it was very depressing. Despite the appalling weather, over 125,000

fans jammed round the circuit for what turned into the most dramatic race of the year – for all the wrong reasons. When the spray finally settled after the 20-lap 500cc race, neither Freddie nor Eddie had increased their World Championship points standings and both had sampled the hard wet tarmac at very close quarters.

After testing the difficult conditions when he won the earlier 250cc race after a five-man battle in which Lavado crashed, Freddie did not manage a single lap in the vital 500 encounter. He saw his championship lead blown apart as he slid along the ground after being brought down by Sarron a mile from the start.

'I'd outbraked Didier de Radigues round the first right-hander lining up for the next left-

First lap of the 500cc Dutch TT. In the first picture Ron Haslam (Honda) leads Didier de Radigues (Honda) into the corner ahead of Spencer but Christian Sarron is already in trouble on his Yamaha (no.6) . . . . mayhem follows as Sarron goes down and slides into Spencer, forcing de Radigues wide . . . Sarron slides ahead while Spencer sits up. On the next page, Freddie has come to rest right in front of photographer Henk Keulemans. A discussion as to Sarron's tactics follows . . .

hander. There was a lot of spray about and all of a sudden I was down on the ground sliding along on top of Sarron's bike. I hardly touched the ground and I ran over to my machine in the mud, but I could not get it out of gear and so I was out.'

The Marlboro Yamaha camp could not believe their luck and Lawson's pit board told him of the situation as he peered through the spray. He was just 7 points down in the championship, so if he finished fourth or above

he would regain his lead. Instead he blew it, making the most important mistake of his entire career.

With that championship lead beckoning he had just snatched second place from Haslam on the ninth lap when he got the front wheel of his Yamaha on a slippery white line surrounding the track and crashed spectacularly, sliding for nearly 100 yards on the grass before picking himself up to start that long, cold, wet walk back to the paddock, where bravely he blamed

101

Freddie finishes fourth in a rain-sodden 250cc race at Silverstone to clinch the 250cc World Championship. Later in the day he stormed to a clear-cut 500cc victory.

nobody but himself.

'I can make no excuses. I just got the front wheel on the white line,' he explained as his fellow Californian Randy Mamola went on to win the race. 'I think you can excuse me for my first mistake in three years of Grand Prix racing.'

During the next six weeks he must have often looked back and reflected on that one mistake as Freddie made the most of being let off the hook and won the next four 500cc Grands Prix. He was also beginning to run away with the 250cc class and had set his sights on clinching the championship at the British Grand Prix, at Silverstone, at the beginning of August.

At the eighth round of the championship at Spa-Francorchamps, in Belgium, he was a comfortable winner of both races. Lawson

made a dreadful start in the 20-lap 500cc race and rode brilliantly through the field to finish second, but he knew it was just not enough as Freddie had increased his lead to 10 points once again.

The 250cc pundits were beginning to reflect that their once very competitive class was becoming more than a little boring as Freddie cruised to victory. He now led the championship by a massive 34 points and the likes of Mang, Lavado and Wimmer did not possess the hardware to stop him.

In the French Grand Prix, at Le Mans, first Australian Wayne Gardner and then Sarron pushed him hard in the 500cc race, but both fell by the wayside in their challenge. Gardner had swapped the lead with him for the opening 13 laps until retiring with rear tyre problems, while

Racing in the rain. Freddie heads for victory in the 500cc British Grand Prix at Silverstone – a success that put him just one win away from clinching the double.

Sarron crashed when he took over the challenge.

Once again Lawson had trouble starting his Marlboro Yamaha and had to ride from the very back to finish fourth, and the World Championship gap was up to 17 points with just three rounds remaining.

Nothing was going to stop Freddie winning the 250cc Championship as he toyed with the opposition once again before clearing off from Mang. He looked certain to clinch the title at Silverstone, just two weeks later.

It was hard to believe it could rain any harder or more frequently than it did at Assen, but

Silverstone proved that particular theory wrong. So heavy was the rain throughout the day that the sidecar race had to be cancelled. However, the rain mattered little to Freddie as he clinched the first part of the unique 'double' by winning the 250cc World Championship when he finished a calculated fourth in the race.

In the appalling conditions his pit signals told him fourth place was enough for the title, and so he just tried to keep out of trouble during the 24 incident-packed laps.

'Those must have been the worst conditions I've ever raced in,' he revealed, while going round on the back of a lorry on his victory lap. 'I

didn't enjoy the race and I wanted to go slower, but I knew I had to finish fourth to win the title. I got involved with a bunch of guys and so I had to keep going.'

Mang won the race, but typically there was not time for celebrations in the Spencer camp. He changed his leathers and boots and jumped onto the 500 to continue his battle with Lawson and the conditions.

The Californian knew his hard-won title was slipping from his grasp and he put in a tremendous effort to halt the slide, but the masterful display in the torrential rain and gale-force winds by Freddie was final proof that

I've done it! Freddie signals his delight after winning the 500cc race in Sweden to regain the heavyweight title and make it a 250cc/ 500cc double.

nobody could, or was capable of, stopping him realize that 'double' dream.

He won the race by over 8 seconds and led the championship by 20 points with two rounds remaining. It was going to be the Anderstorp circuit, in Sweden, on which he had won that dramatic confrontation two years earlier with Kenny Roberts, that would provide the stage for the final act, just seven days later.

A day after his Silverstone victory Freddie was on the Terry Wogan TV chat show. It is one of the most popular shows on British television, and his appearance just demonstrated the thin line that professional motorcycle racers tread.

Shaded by his sponsor's umbrellas Spencer and his right hand man Iain "Mac" Mackay celebrate in Sweden but the festivities ended with a splash (opposite) when Spencer, aided by a Honda mechanic, finished up in the swimming pool.

Just three days earlier, on a wild and windy Friday morning, he was blown from his 250 Honda at Copse corner. He was not injured, but one cracked bone would have wrecked the 'double' chances and certainly Terry Wogan would not have played host.

As is often the case, the actual hour of victory after months of continual pressure and work channelled into one direction, turned out a bit of an anti-climax. It is only when people start unwinding that they realize just what they have achieved, and the Swedish race, at Anderstorp, proved one of those occasions.

Having clinched the title, Freddie missed the 250 race on the Saturday and watched from the stands as Mang won his second Grand Prix in succession. Freddie was in pole position for the 30-lap 500cc race, which was held in the dry, after rain had fallen on the earlier 125cc race.

From the moment he took the lead on the second lap there was never much doubt about the outcome as he reeled off 75 immaculate miles of mastery. Lawson was lucky to finish second when Gardner, who had relegated him to third place, ran out of petrol on the last lap.

After the ritual throwing in the swimming pool ceremony, a relaxed Freddie and Sarie packed up their belongings and caught the evening plane to London to prepare for a massive Rothmans press conference two days later.

'It was a little touch-and-go in the morning when it was pouring with rain,' he explained on the flight from Gothenburg as he celebrated with a soft drink (although he'd bought champagne for all the journalists), 'But it dried up for the race and I made the right choice of tyres. The only problem was the strong wind. It

was important to make a good start, which I did, behind Ron Haslam and Didier de Radigues. Once I took the lead on the second lap I was able to set a comfortable pace and ease away from Eddie.'

He missed the final Grand Prix of the season when he injured his thumb and hand during weight training and so for the third time in four seasons, his racing year ended prematurely because of injury.

Then, when he came back for a late-season Japanese race, he crashed while practising at Suzuka at 120mph. The NSR Honda was completely burnt out in the crash and Freddie flew home with ligament injuries to both feet and abrasions to his legs, elbows and hands.

While at home with family and friends he slowly unwound and the feeling of satisfaction and pride at becoming the first rider to ever achieve the 250cc and 500cc World Championship 'double' began to sink in.

'It was a hard season for everybody. We all put everything into it, and when you achieve something like that it takes a while to enjoy it,' he explained. 'It's all a bit anti-climatic for a while because you've worked so hard to achieve it. You know, I enjoy it more now than I did a week ago, and a whole lot more than I did two weeks ago.'

One of each – Freddie Spencer indicates his intentions after winning both 250cc and 500cc races at Mugello. By the end of the 1985 season he had become the first rider to win both World Championships in the same year.

FAST FREDDIE

THE MACHINES

By Peter Clifford

Freddie Spencer has always maintained that his machines and those who prepare them are vital to his success. Developing the bikes through work on the suspension, weight distribution and engine tuning forms a major part of his racing effort and as the machines have become more and more sophisticated so this has taken more of his time.

Spencer has relied a great deal on Erv Kanemoto throughout his National and International two-stroke racing experience since his father gave up being his mechanic. Kanemoto remembers how the relationship started: 'His father came to me in 1978 and asked me to do some work on his 250cc Yamaha engine. I knew that he was already doing very well and felt that rather than sell him the work I would do him some cylinders which he could use and he finished the second half of his novice season with them.'

Kanemoto already had an enviable reputation not only as an engine tuner, but as a frame builder and for the following season he built a special Yamaha-based machine for Spencer to use. Kanemoto had been working with Gary Nixon and the pair had contested the 1976 Formula 750 World Championship with a Kawasaki triple for which Kanemoto had built a special frame using larger than standard diameter tubing to increase the rigidity.

He then turned his attention to the 750cc Yamaha four and prepared one for Nixon to use in 1977. It was a bike that Spencer would also get to ride and the 750cc Yamaha proved a very important motorcycle, not only for Spencer, but for many other riders over a decade of racing.

The TZ750 Yamaha could trace its ancestry back to a 500cc across-the-frame four-cylinder two-stroke that the famous Finn Jarno Saarinen raced for the factory in 1973. After the initial success of the 500 in Saarinen's hands, Yamaha decided to build a 750 version for 1974 and to sell it around the world as an out-and-out racing machine that anyone could buy. They retained the 54mm stroke of the 500, but increased the bore to 64mm as used on their 350cc twins to give a capacity of 694cc. The machine made its debut at Daytona in March 1974. Like the 500 it had reed valves which kept the power docile and flexible, making the 90bhp

it developed very usable. These TZ750s outclassed the opposition with Giacomo Agostini, having his first ride for Yamaha, winning from Kenny Roberts.

By the time Nixon gave up racing the Kawasaki in 1977 the Yamaha was dominating road-racing in the States and in Formula 750 and other International events in Europe. Kanemoto worked his magic on the Yamaha and made his TZ750 faster than anything but the works OW31 versions ridden by Kenny Roberts and unavailable to the privateer.

Yamaha TZ 750

In 1979 Spencer was only 17 at the start of the American season and because of his age was unable to compete in National events, but he rode the TZ750 at some club races with devastating effect. It was when Spencer first tested the TZ750 that Kanemoto was left in no doubt as to what incredible possibilities there were for the young rider: 'He just jumped on it and went as quick as anyone,' remembers Kanemoto. 'We were running restrictors in the 750s at the time, but I ran the bike without for the test session to see just how he would cope with the sudden power surge. He took to it immediately. Before that I had thought it was just possible that he had limitations. The press were saying that here was a guy who had been racing since he was six, so I wondered if it was like watching a guy who had 10 years' experience. He was so smooth that he was either a genius or he had reached his peak and was just very comfortable. You kind of expect that riders who are on the way up and really trying will look out of shape sometimes. He didn't. That is why I put him on the 750 without restrictors. It was not easy to ride. It was so powerful it would spin the rear tyre anywhere, but it did not give him any problems. It was then I knew he would be able to take on anything and adapt to any race track or motorcycle.'

Spencer got his chance to race the TZ750 at his first National, which was Daytona in March 1980. There he was up against the factory OW31 Yamaha with Roberts aboard and the bike needed all the speed Kanemoto could give it. The frame Erv had made himself. It looked like the standard TZ750, with similar engine position and steering geometry, but was built using better material, chrome-moly steel, and was stiffer and stronger than the standard unit.

Part of Kanemoto's tuning logic was to get cool fresh air to the carburettors. This is a common enough consideration now, but at that time few people paid any attention to it. The Yamaha had its four carburettors facing rearward behind the cylinders. They were likely to breathe warm air that had passed through the radiator and over the engine. Worse still, one of the exhaust pipes was routed around the side of the engine and across the face of the carburettor intake bellmouths.

Kanemoto had some plastic ducting positioned to deflect the heat and give the carburettors cool air to breathe. It certainly seemed to help, and Spencer's bike was the only one that could stay anywhere near Roberts' during practice at Daytona. Oddly, Kanemoto suggests that it was the ducting that may have cost Spencer the race as he retired with a failed

crank while leading: 'Freddie had to pass on the dirt early on and I think some grit got sucked into the engine because it was a low-mileage crank and should easily have gone the distance.' Spencer got a second chance to show how good the Kanemoto 750 was in the Anglo-American Match races, and he did so with a vengeance.

Spencer was obviously a star in the making and there was pressure on him to accomplish everything at once, and so a Grand Prix was pencilled into his race calendar. The only problem was that there was no 500 for him to ride. He had the TZ750 Yamaha plus the Honda 1000 Superbike and Formula One machines, but no 500cc racer suitable for World Championship Grand Prix racing.

Yamaha TZ500

The team tried to borrow a works machine, but none was available on a one-off basis so he and Kanemoto were forced to use a production Yamaha. It, like the TZ750, could trace its

Erv Kanemoto wheels out the production Yamaha that Spencer (right) used for his European Grand Prix debut at Zolder in Belgium in 1980.

parentage back to the factory 500, but by this time the factory machine being raced by Kenny Roberts in the World Championships had the cylindrical exhaust valves, which effectively altered the exhaust port timing to give the engine more flexibility.

Johnny Cecotto first used an engine fitted with such cylinders in the Venezuelan Grand Prix at the beginning of 1978, but Roberts was the rising star and soon got to use the better engines on his way to his first world title. At various Grands Prix through the 1979 season Japanese test-riders used simplified versions of the factory YZR500 which was to be the first 500cc Yamaha racer sold to the public. Instead of the electronically controlled, electric motor-actuated valves fitted to the works bikes, these had comparatively crude centrifugal drives powered from the end of the crankshaft by a flexible cable.

Yamaha produced these machines as a counter to the dominance of Grand Prix racing by the RG500 Suzuki which was used by almost all privateers. Only the works Yamahas could beat them and because Roberts had, by the end of 1979, won two titles, these supposed replicas were at first in great demand.

The rear swing arm was fabricated from aluminium sheet and rectangular-section tubing. It was strong enough, but the single unit for the cantilever suspension was not the same as the unit fitted to the works bikes and it showed. The frame was a simple twin loop steel design with insufficient cross-bracing and not as well supported by the engine as on the TZ750. Additionally, the front forks were not strong enough – the main tubes being 36mm diameter compared to the 40mm used by Suzuki.

Even more than the TZ750, the 500 needed the advantages of a Kanemoto frame, but there was no time to build it as they only got the bike in time for Spencer to test it at Laguna Seca a week before his Grand Prix debut in Belgium.

Unlike the TZ750, the 500 had individual cylinders, and instead of through studs from the crankcase that ran all the way to the heads, the 500 had short studs just through the base of the cylinders and separate head bolts. This gave more room for the transfer ports in the cylinders, which had a bore of 56mm and a stroke of 50.7mm.

Once the cylinders were removed the crankcase cover could come off. This again was different to the 750, whose cases were split right through the centre of the crank and clutch. The 500 had a separate gearbox all-in-one casting and the internals were removed through a side cover. Once the 500's crank cover was removed the two separate cranks were in full view. Split into two pressed cranks, they were splined to a gear, which drove a jackshaft running across to the right-hand side of the engine, where it drove the clutch. The side-loading gearbox allowed quick and easy changing of the ratios to suit different circuits.

The 500 crank was much stronger than the 750, thanks to the fact that the gears were splined instead of held by a key and the middle section of each pair forged in one piece like a dumbell. The clutch was much smaller and lighter than the 750 and ran faster to help it cope with the power.

The Yamaha looked promising in specification, but in practice it was no match for the faster private RG500s, never mind the works machines. Cecotto rode one in the first GP of 1980 at Misano and finished a good fourth, but in Spain he was sixth behind Sheene on a similar machine, and at Paul Ricard, Cecetto dropped to ninth.

At least the machines were finishing in the top 10 and at the Dutch TT Jack Middelburg won in tricky conditions using a Yamaha engine fitted into a Nico Bakker frame. That was part of the Yamaha's problem. The frame was too weak and Sheene had already asked British frame-makers Harris to build a special unit for him.

Spencer arrived at Zolder in Belgium with an almost standard machine. The tests at Laguna had demonstrated the fact that the bike did not handle well and they bought with them a set of Marzocchi forks. Kanemoto hoped they would help, but they were tried and then discarded.

Zolder was the last place to ride a bike with poor handling because the surface had been torn and rippled by Formula One cars. Kanemoto says that the circuit and the handling were not their greatest problem as Spencer had

The Yamaha production racer of 1980 was no match for the RG500 Suzuki of the day. Here Erv Kanemoto works on the machine that Spencer rode at Zolder that year.

the ability to make up for so much. It was the engine that really made them suffer: 'I had made some more exhaust pipes for it and we had Lectron carburettors because there was so much lag in the standard Mikunis, but there was just no time to get the bike sorted out.'

The weather did not help. It was damp for most of the time and the carburation was way out for the race: 'It is no good now, but I wish we could go back to Zolder because no-one saw Freddie as they should have. The bike was just so rich it would not rev. If we had just had one more clear day to sort out the carburation I think the result would have been very different. We had gone there with the intention of doing well and it was a disappointment to me'.

After Zolder, Spencer and Kanemoto returned to the States where they continued to campaign the TZ750 in National races and at the same time Freddie rode the American Honda Superbike.

US Superbike

To understand the Superbikes as Freddie Spencer rode them it is interesting to consider briefly the history of the class in the USA. The first AMA race for production machines was held at Laguna Seca in 1973 and the rules were based on the club regulations that already existed. Engine modifications were limited to cams, pistons and gearing. The carburettors and gearboxes as well as frames, wheels and exhaust systems had to remain standard.

The rules evolved as competition grew fiercer. Engine tuning and the use of wider racing tyres and rims and close-ratio gearboxes

Honda signed Fast Freddie to race their Superbike in 1980. Here he is with the machine he raced at Daytona that year.

The Honda team at Daytona in 1980. Left to right: Ron Pierce, Roberto Petri, Freddie Spencer and team-manager Steve McLaughlin.

led away from production racing to the point in 1976 where the AMA changed the name to Superbike Production. The new rules allowed racing exhausts, almost unlimited engine modification and complete freedom with suspension, wheels and brakes within the limitations of frame strengthening rather than replacement, plus a requirement that the silhouette of the machine resemble the original road bike so that the original seat and tank as well as handlebar position had to be retained.

Kawasaki were the first Japanese factory to get interested in the class. In 1979 they hired Mike Baldwin to ride for them, though Baldwin was still more interested in the pukka racers they also had to offer. Yoshimura, the famous tuning company, were also getting in on the act running Suzukis.

At the time Spencer's Superbike was a rather uncompetitive Ducati, but he was then offered a ride by Kawasaki after the Loudon National where Baldwin broke his leg. Spencer was teamed with Richard Schlachter and first raced the KZ at Sears Point after testing the bike only two days before the event. He blitzed the field, opening up a huge lead after only a few laps and then cruised to victory. He repeated the win at Laguna Seca the following weekend.

The class was beginning to boom and that got Honda interested. The spectators were excited at the idea of watching bikes that looked like those they rode competing out on the track. Honda wanted the best so they signed Spencer for the 1980 season. Kawasaki chose the one man who had been anything like competitive with Spencer, Eddie Lawson.

It seems that it was a fairly late decision for Honda to go Superbike racing in 1980 and the team only met for the first time on January 15 to start getting their bikes together for the opening race at Daytona in early March.

The bike had to be based on a roadster and that meant the CB750F. Fortunately a similar powerplant had been used as the basis of the

117

factory 1000cc endurance and British Formula One racers. This meant there was a 996.5cc kit available from the RSC racing services side of the factory who supplied much of the equipment required, including dry clutch, ignition, close-ratio gearbox, dry sump and oil-cooling system.

Honda America chose a different path in the carburettor department and employed the latest offerings from stateside carb expert Bill Edmonston in the form of some very special Blue Magnum flat-slide carbs, painted blue to distinguish them from Lectrons. These had externally adjustable metering rods, making fine tuning of the fuel and air mixture very easy, a big help to pit-road tuning.

Although the main loop of the frame had to be retained, the demands of racing required that the steering geometry be altered and the tubes round the headstock were cut, bent and rewelded to bring the head back about an inch at the top, which kicked the fork angle out and increased the self-centring effect of the steering. This was done because with the standard steering head and racing tyres the front-end tended to tuck under or push going into corners.

In fact the steering geometry changed a good deal. Front forks from the massive Gold Wing GL1000 tourer were fitted, which were a good deal more robust. These were made to work reasonably well by partially closing off some of the damper holes to increase the compression damping and thus resist their tendency to collapse under braking. The forks were also strengthened by fitting bigger-than-usual yokes.

The braking was taken care of by Lockheed calipers, two on the front and one at the rear. Two huge 13in Mehanite drilled discs were mounted on Morris Magnesium wheels fitted with Goodyear tyres; 19in at the front and 18 at the rear.

The rear wheel was held in a swing arm reinforced by a box-section addition and the strengthening was continued through the frame, above the swing-arm pivot, above the front engine-mount and around the backbone that ran under the tank from the steering head. More suspension travel was gained by moving the top unit mountings so that the shocks lay further forward.

With oil but no fuel the 1980 Superbike weighed some 414lb and American Honda did a good deal of their own tuning work to the twin-cam 16-valve engine. The power, reputed to be close to 140bhp, was taken through a 14-plate four-spring dry clutch, which replaced the larger diameter 16-plate wet clutch of the road bike. This was an RSC component and the new backing plate and cover were cast in magnesium to keep the weight down. The Superbike was producing much more power than the endurance racers, and riders had to go easy on the clutch.

Engine width was minimized thanks to the RSC electrical system, which used a constant loss 12-volt battery and only two small triggers, mounted next to the end of the crank, and two amplifiers and coils. The bulky generator was discarded.

Though the development time was very limited, the bike was good enough for Spencer to finish second to Graeme Crosby in its first outing on March 7 at Daytona, and Ron Pierce on another of the team's machines was third. Crosby rode the Yoshimura Suzuki Superbike and Yoshimura had had a full season of development in 1979.

Spencer won on the Honda at the beginning of June at Elkhart Lake, then again at Loudon and Laguna Seca. He was second when the Championship returned to Daytona at the end of the year, following Wes Cooley (Yoshimura Suzuki) across the line in a photo-finish.

The Honda team were plagued with con-rod failures during the season and this, together with tyre problems, dropped Spencer to third in the Championship behind Cooley and Lawson.

For 1981 Spencer was committed to ride the Honda four-strokes in both the Superbike and Formula One classes. Honda built special machines for the F1 class using similar engines to the superbike, but with full race frames and fairings. The capacity limit was 1,025cc and they raced against 500cc Grand Prix two-strokes and the TZ750 Yamahas, though the big two-strokes were handicapped by having to fit 23mm inlet restrictors that kept the power down and made the class more even.

Spencer's 1980 Daytona Superbike in the workshop – the 1,000cc race-prepared engine developed nearly 140bhp.

Honda retained the slightly old-fashioned twin-shock rear suspension on Spencer's Formula One bike, keeping the wheelbase short at 55 inches (1 inch shorter than a 750 Yamaha, 3 inches shorter than the Honda Superbike and shorter than the Pro Link endurance racers). The European long-distance machines used the Pro Link suspension, which placed the single unit in front of the rear wheel, necessitating a longer wheelbase. Team-mate Roberto Pietri used a Harris Performance chassis with adjustable rocker-arm rear suspension after racing one at Brands Hatch at the end of the 1980 season. Japanese engineer Ron Murakami was in charge of the racing development at the time and pointed out that the size of the 1,025cc four-stroke engine virtually dictated the location of all components. To get a short enough chassis for good handling the rear tyre had to be chewing at the back of the gearbox, while the headers of the exhaust pipes had to be touching the front tyre at full deflection.

To get the old-fashioned twin-shock arrangement to work well they needed some good units. Mike Baldwin, who had joined the team halfway through 1980 after a 14-month layoff suggested the use of Ohlins rear units. These had a well-deserved reputation in motocross, though at that time they were uncommon in road-racing. The team adopted them with great results.

The units had to handle a bike fitted with a 172lb engine and with a rolling chassis weight of 243lb in the case of the Superbike and 198lb for the Formula One. They competed against TZ750 Yamahas whose engines weighed in at 140lb and chassis at 195lb.

Though the Superbikes retained the roadster forks, now the 39mm diameter units from the latest GL1100 tourers, the Formula One bikes had 41.3mm units built by Showa for the endurance and European F1 racers. Udo Gietl looked after the engines, which had dry sumps, and he fitted titanium valves. They had a choice of American EI flat-slide or Japanese Keihin carbs and alternative ratios for the gearbox with four possible primary ratios plus alternatives for first, fourth and fifth.

Kawasaki were not standing still though, and their American team had persuaded the factory to produce their 1981 1,000cc Kawasaki roadsters with frames to Superbike specifications complete with re-angled steering head, backbone triangulation and extra cross-members. They also had a few parts from the factory Grand Prix effort to use on the Superbikes including some superb four-piston brake calipers. Engine power was Kawasaki's problem and they had to work hard, while Honda claimed that their engines were producing a massive 135bhp.

At Daytona in 1981 Spencer's Formula One bike blew up while he had a comfortable lead. The team suggested that the engine had ingested some spilt fuel at the refuelling stop and that the incompressible fluid had caused a bent con-rod. His bike had looked incredibly fast, though, and blasted past the Yoshimura Suzuki of Wes Cooley with a massive display of horsepower. The Suzuki had always been one of the fastest and so shocked was John Ulrich, then reporting for *Cycle News*, that he put forward the possibility that the machine had employed bursts of nitrous oxide injection. Injection of the power-giving, oxygen-rich substance is often used in drag racing and was not specifically banned under AMA road-race regulations.

Spencer won on the Formula One bike in the next race at Elkhart Lake, but the next time he raced in that class was at Laguna Seca, when

Honda wheeled out the Grand Prix NR500 for him to use. He even beat Kenny Roberts on the GP Yamaha in a heat, though the bike stopped in the main 100km event. It gave Honda a tremendous boost with a machine that had failed dismally in the World Championships since its debut towards the end of the 1979 season. The success meant Spencer was to ride the same bike at Silverstone for the British Grand Prix.

Honda NR500

The NR500 project was shrouded in secrecy from beginning to end. Honda's management announced to the world in December 1977 that they would return to Grand Prix racing with a 500cc four-stroke and it is said that until then the engineers who would design and build the machine knew nothing of the plan. That seems unlikely, but the prospect of building a competitive four-stroke was daunting, to say the least, particularly as the FIM regulations had changed since Honda pulled out at the end of the 1967 season, limiting 500cc machines to a maximum of four cylinders.

In decreeing that they must use a four-stroke engine the head of the company placed his engineers at a great disadvantage, for the two-stroke has twice as many power strokes for a given number of revolutions. Honda really needed to be able to build an eight-cylinder engine if they were to stand any real chance of matching the four-cylinder two-stokes for power.

What Honda did was to build a 'four' that attempted to use some of the advantages of an eight-cylinder engine; namely the greater inlet efficiency offered by more valves. As they could not use a four-valves-per-cylinder V8 they built an eight-valves-per-cylinder V4!

Fitting that many valves into a cylinder could not be done readily in a normal circular bore. So Honda developed a bore with semi-circular ends and straight sides which could accommodate eight valves neatly (viewed from above, the piston's shape is like a running track or squashed oval).

The machines made their racing debut at Silverstone in 1979, ending a 12-year absence by Honda from GP racing. But the bikes were a

The first version of the ill-fated four-stroke racer appeared in 1979.

disaster for many reasons. They were slow and the aluminium monocoque frames cracked with frustrating frequency.

By the time Freddie Spencer raced the bike at Laguna Seca in 1981 the engine was into at least its third total redesign and it shared little more than the number of cylinders with the original layout. The monocoque frame was long gone and had been replaced by a very conventional twin-loop tubular steel design.

One of the problems with the powerplant was that as the throttle was closed the engine had so much braking it almost stopped dead. Later

versions were fitted with a special clutch that allowed a degree of freewheel on the overrun thanks to a one-way partial slip system. It was later developed for use on road machines.

The NR engine still had eight valves per cylinder and revved to 20,000rpm, but the angle between the cylinders had been reduced to 90 degrees with one pair of cylinders horizontal and the other vertical. The crank was a pressed unit with two con-rods for each piston, to stop the odd-shaped lumps rocking in the bores, and needle-roller main bearings. At least one of the engines had 19mm inlet and 17mm exhaust

Another shot of the early NR500 – taken at the French Grand Prix at Le Mans. The machine in the centre has been "split" – the complete engine and rear section unbolted and wheeled out of the monocoque chassis.

valves, but the exact specification of all the engines remains a secret.

The engines may not have been successful, but they were a work of art and the two banks of carburettors with their eight chokes were a masterful piece of miniature work. The heads had two minute spark plugs for each cylinder to give a more rapid burn across the very broad combustion chamber.

Spencer rode the machine hard at the British Grand Prix at Silverstone in 1981. He needed to as it was obviously not competitive. The rev limit on the machine was 22,000rpm, but at that the engines were well known to be very short-fused. Spencer was asked to keep to well below so that the engine would finish the race.

He obviously had a straight choice. Ride carefully and finish, like Katayama had done before, out of the points and unimpressive, or rev the heart out of the NR and see what happened. He was up into fifth place when the engine blew-up early on. Spencer had made his choice and he certainly impressed many people with the performance.

One of the most important things that happened at Silverstone where Spencer rode the NR was that he saw Kanemoto again. Erv had left the USA to work with Barry Sheene in Europe for 1981 and when they met at the British Grand Prix Spencer asked the ace engineer to work with him on the Grand Prix Honda in 1982.

This final version of the NR500 with carbon fibre frame was never raced and used only as a show attraction. The project cost Honda millions of pounds and delayed their successful return to racing by four years.

The preparation of the machine requires a constant dialogue between Freddie Spencer and Erv Kanemoto who translates his diagnoses into mechanical adjustments.

Kanemoto readily agreed as it was precisely what he wanted and things were working out perfectly for the pair of them because Kanemoto now had a season of Grand Prix experience behind him: 'I had decided that I needed to spend a year in Europe so that later no-one would be able to say I lacked experience in that area. It was a good opportunity when Sheene asked me to work with him, but I knew it would only be for a limited period. I didn't feel I needed to learn that much about the racing. It

was the living I needed to learn about. I had to be exposed to it. During that year I realized that though I preferred to live at home in America I could cope with it. It was important to me to be asked to work with Freddie as I felt I could contribute something to the effort both with the living in Europe and the technical work with the machine. You can throw him on a bike and he will do something incredible; like a lot of talented people he compensates to make the best of whatever is given to him. I felt I could

124

Spencer looks on while mechanics work on his NS500 three-cylinder racer.

give him options on the machine which could allow him to go further,' said Erv.

In the Autumn of 1981 Kanemoto first saw the NS500 two-stroke: 'I was surprised that it was powered by a three-cylinder reed-valve engine, but all the research was well founded. Honda had looked at the possibilities of reed-valve engines logically and what they produced was like a high-powered 350 with the advantages of minimal size and weight. We had gone to Japan to test it, but it was not ready and was later shipped to Laguna Seca in December. After that we went to Interlagos, in Brazil, for more testing before the first race in Argentina.

Honda NS500

Honda were determined to expunge the bitter memories of the NR defeat and put all their massive resources behind the new two-stroke project. They knew that even with a two-stroke, winning would not be easy as they faced the

three other Japanese factories, each planning a full-scale Grand Prix campaign. Suzuki had their well-tried and constantly developing disc-valve, square-four. Yamaha also had a square-four engine, with a V4 rumoured to be waiting in the wings, while Kawasaki completed the opposition with another square-four.

In the days of their earlier domination of the Grand Prix scene in the 1960s, Honda had often relied on complex engines to beat the opposition, with more cylinders and more valves. The number of cylinders was now restricted to four, but Honda could have been expected at least to match the opposition.

What they did surprised many. They produced an engine with fewer moving parts than any of the others. A V3 with reed-valve induction that did not even have revolutionary porting. It was as if they had cobbled up a 500 out of three motocross engines.

There was a good reason for this. The man in

Mechanics work on Freddie's NS500 three-cylinder at the German Grand Prix in 1984 for which it was brought out of retirement to win.

charge of the new project was Shinichi Miyakoshi, an engineer who had developed several of Honda's very successful single-cylinder, reed-valve motocrossers. He realized the advantages of such an arrangement; the savings in weight and internal friction.

To take full advantage of the layout the three cylinders were placed in a 110-degree vee. This allowed Honda to use a single, four-bearing crank, saving four bearings and a crank over the fours. Honda also avoided the drag of the disc valves and used their considerable knowledge of reed-valve development to control the flow of charge in and out of the cylinders. The bore and stroke was well over-square at 62.6mm X 54mm, giving a capacity of 498.7cc.

The primary drive was taken off the left-hand end of the crank and transmitted through two gears of the same size to a layshaft that ran back across the engine to the clutch. This shaft

helped damp out vibration and passed the drive to the dry clutch on the right-hand side. From behind the clutch the gearbox internals could be removed and changed.

The first NS500s had steel frames, aluminium wheels and battery ignition. By the Dutch TT in 1982 lighter aluminium frames had replaced the steel units and carbon-fibre wheels were being used. These retained the cast magnesium hubs, but the aluminium rims and separate spokes were replaced by carbon-fibre.

For 1983 the ignition system was changed to dispense with the battery. It was replaced by a self-generating unit on the left-hand end of the crank. Power was aided by the addition of the ATAC system that varied the exhaust pipe volume.

Honda had developed the ATAC system on various off-road machines, but it was

126

something new to employ it on a road-racer. Its job was to make the engine more flexible by broadening the power band. It did this by altering the volume of the exhaust sytem. A butterfly valve increased the volume at low revs so that the engine would drive from lower down. This increased the three-cylinder machine's already apparent advantage in getting the power on to the ground. Accelerating out of the corners, the rival four-cylinder Yamahas spun their rear wheels and slid sideways while the Honda laid a black rubber mark driving forward.

Though the NS lacked power early in 1982, things improved as work was done on the cylinders and exhausts, so that by the beginning of the 1983 season the Honda was the best all-round machine. This was crucial to the results for the year. The square-four disc-valve Suzuki was on the wane. The Suzuki factory had concentrated on making each new model lighter and more compact than the forerunner. They won the title in 1981 and 1982 working to this plan but eventually the engine became so small that it could not breathe properly.

Yamaha had used their disc-valve V4 early in 1982, but it had handled badly because of a combination of frame and power-band problems. It was still not right at the beginning of 1983 and the machine was very hard to start. Carburation remained a problem and the bike was obviously not as easy to ride as the Honda.

One of the less obvious changes made to the 1983 NS was to lower the machine and alter the weight distribution so that it did not push the front-end quite as hard as it had done in the previous year. Even with the ATAC boxes, which were only used on the upper two cylinders, the power band required accurate choice of gearbox internals. After a year of experience with the machine and thanks to the various improvements, Kanemoto recalls that they were most often on top of the situation: 'In '83 we went to the line with a bike that was on the day better than the opposition had. In some ways the Honda was simpler to work with. The Yamaha did have more power, but it seemed to come in fairly hard and that made it a sort of trade-off. There were places where the Yamaha was better – Austria and Silverstone for

example – but the Honda was the best balanced machine on the race track. At Silverstone we were more than happy to finish second, it was almost like winning there.'

At other circuits the NS500 was more suitable, and it really impressed in Belgium, where Spencer made use of its handling and flexibility through the corners: 'At Spa we lapped faster than the Yamaha. Kenny was three-quarters of a second faster on the uphill climb where the power of the Yamaha told, but Freddie was three-quarters of a second faster over the whole lap, so he was making up one and a half seconds over the twisty sections,' said Erv later.

Kanemoto remembers that there were many things that contributed to winning the World Championship in 1983: 'Michelin had been working hard with the tyres through the winter and that helped to stop the front pushing the way it had in 1982. It was also very important that we managed to guess right about which engine to use several times. The other one might fail in practice at the next track; luck was with us, Honda kept working on the development and the best engine we had was at Imola at the end of the season, when Freddie only had to finish second to Kenny.'

Spencer remembers well the help the new powerplant gave him at that last race of the season: 'The engine had a better power-band than it had ever had before. It meant that I could use the power to pull the front-end round and prevent it from sliding away.' That made it easier for him to take the 12 points he needed to win the Championship.

Though the NS500 three-cylinder had won the Championship the team knew that they needed something faster for the 1984 season. Kanemoto remembers: 'The Yamaha was getting better all the time and we had a meeting to decide what was needed. It was obvious that a four-cylinder engine was required because we had to have more power.'

Honda NSR500

After developing the incredibly successful NS500 on which Freddie Spencer won the

Racing is a year-long business – here Freddie tests the NSR500 four-cylinder at Surfers Paradise in Australia in December 1983.

1983 World Championship Honda felt that they had to replace it with a more advanced machine to give Spencer the best possible chance of retaining the title the following year, particularly as Yamaha were improving their V4 all the time.

The problem was that replacing such a well-balanced machine is not easy and so rather than simply equipping the 1983 chassis with a 'four' producing more power they decided to try and take several steps forward at the same time. That was their mistake.

Freddie Spencer tested two prototype versions of the new V4 NSR500 at Surfers Paradise in Australia in December 1983. Both had the petrol tank mounted under the engine, a novel innovation as far as a Japanese factory team is concerned, though it had been tried by smaller constructors before.

One machine had a conventional twin-loop frame in square-section aluminium tubing like the three-cylinder, but the bike that Spencer

eventually raced used a frame fabricated from pressed aluminium sections forming two main spars, one running either side of the engine and reinforced by tubes that ran down from the steering head to form what Honda call a Diamond Back frame.

The idea behind putting the petrol tank underneath was to lower the centre of gravity, but it caused problems when it came to positioning everything else. The exhaust pipes had to go over the top of the engine and this created a number of heat problems. The engine ran 10 degrees hotter than the 'three' and suffered a good number of carburation problems that may have been partly due to the engine breathing hot air, despite Honda's attempts to duct fresh air to a chamber around the carburettors.

Trying to sort out the carburation proved a nightmare for the mechanics because working on the carburettors meant removing the exhaust-pipes. The fact that the engine and

The 1984 version of the NSR500 four-cylinder had the exhaust pipes running over the top of the engine with the fuel carried in a low-slung belly tank. Although theoretically a good idea, it did not work out in practice.

The 1985 version of the NSR500 four-cylinder reverted to a conventional layout. Here mechanics prepare to fit the bank of four carburettors to the crankcase of Spencer's machine.

pipes were hot made everything else hot as well: 'Even the fairing screws were too hot to touch,' commented one mechanic. 'Having to take the pipes off before you could do anything made life very difficult and getting the tank on or off with 20 litres of fuel in it was a two-man job.'

After crashing in practising and not being able to race in the opening Grand Prix in South Africa in 1984, Spencer won on the 'four' in Italy, but then crashed at Donington Park in the Transatlantic match races. When he raced again in Austria the bike proved a headache. Carburation problems and confusing plug readings made it impossible to sort out: 'The engine was just flat,' said Spencer later. 'It just never ran as well as it did the first day. We found out later that we had been deceived by the plug

readings from the engine. Erv had jetted down before we got to Austria knowing that there was less air, but the readings indicated that it was still rich. As we went leaner on the jetting the engine got slower, but it still didn't look lean.'

The next weekend Spencer dramatically reverted to the triple for the German Grand Prix and before long had put himself on pole position: 'I had forgotten just what a good machine the "three" was,' said Spencer, 'especially since the end of last season when we got an engine with a wider spread of power; that made the handling better because the front-end doesn't tend to wash out in the corners. There is enough power to pull it back.'

Pushing the front-end may no longer have been a problem with the triple, but Spencer was

Although Spencer raced the NSR500 four-cylinder in 1985, Honda continued to develop the NS500 three-cylinder. This is the 1985 version as raced by Australian Wayne Gardner and Ron Haslam for Honda UK.

still having handling problems with the NSR: 'The problem with the "four" is that it is such hard work to change direction,' he said. 'I don't know why it is exactly, I'm not sure that putting the petrol tank under the engine is the right move. We had two bikes to test in Australia when I first rode the 'four', but both had tanks underneath so I don't know what it would be like in a conventional position.'

Team-mates Ron Haslam and Randy Mamola also tried the 'four', and though Mamola won the British Grand Prix at Silverstone on one, neither liked it. At the end of 1984 it was completely redesigned with a new frame and conventionally-positioned fuel tank and exhausts. In 1985 Spencer reported it a much better machine to ride: 'It is much easier

to get it from one side to the other, it feels completely different. It seemed on the old bike with the petrol underneath that it was like having a heavy rock on the end of a long stick. It was very difficult to control. Now I have the weight of the petrol much closer to me. You cannot stop the petrol sloshing about completely and with it all down low it just seemed to push the front wheel away. Typical was my fall at Donington at the Match races in '84. When I went into the corner the front-end just dug in. If that had happened on the three-cylinder it would have come back. I know what to do in that situation and I am 95 per cent sure that I could have saved it. On the "four" there was no way I could. The front just dug in like the tip of a vaulting pole.'

Plumbers nightmare! Low level shot shows complex exhaust pipe layout of the 1985 NSR500 four-cylinder.

Right from the first day of practice in South Africa at the start of the season Spencer was happier with the 'four' than he had been all through 1984 but he still had his reservations: 'If I could get the "four" to run as well as the "three" I would be very happy.'

Things continued to improve, but his crash during the untimed warm-up period in Spain when the front tyre slipped away, was proof that everything was not perfect. 'The front-end can tuck under with no warning,' said Spencer. 'That is what happened and there was no chance of saving it. It's what last year's bike did only that was a whole lot worse. We have been working hard on this one and it is getting better. We had the problem in South Africa, combined with some chattering, and the front-end slid away on me then. Now they have moved the engine forward and put more weight on the front, and through practice things got better. We thought we had decided what tyre to use, but then it went and let go on me and I had to go

back to a different one for the race.'

A week later the development took a big step forward during practice for the German Grand Prix. It enabled him to knock 2½ seconds off his practice time in the last session to take pole position with a time nearly 4 seconds quicker than this own lap record! Improvements in the handling allowed him to use the Michelin radial front tyre for the first time. Previously he had been forced to use the older cross-ply construction tyre because the radial would cause the front-end to patter.

'We have been gradually improving the bike all the time, but apart from Daytona we were unable to use the radial front last year or this until now. We have moved the weight distribution and it has really started to work,' said Spencer 'I know the Yamahas have been able to race with it before, but for us the German Grand Prix was the first time.'

It was not just the handling that had been improved over the 18 months of development.

Putting the petrol tank back on top made things easier for the mechanics. The bank of cylindrical-slide carbs became accessible without removing the exhaust pipes, although a small length of seat subframe had to be unbolted to get them out. Engine temperature was lowered because on the 1985 model they did not enclose the engine with plastic and the V-shaped radiator deflected the hot air out through large holes in the fairing.

As in the 1984 engine, the revised NSR500 had reed-valve induction direct into the crankcase and drew air through four carburettor chokes cast in pairs to make them more compact. The reeds were not mounted so that the split between the reed flaps was horizontal, as on most engines including the NS500 triple, but vertically, so that the airflow between the crank flywheels was improved.

At first it is not easy to see how the carburettors were any better served with air

than they were in 1984, but in fact the new machine was fitted with a scoop just behind the bottom of the steering head and this ducted fresh air over the top of the radiator. A complete plastic pan kept this air away from the upward-pointing cylinders and ducted it to an airbox around the carburettors. The underside of the tank completed the ducting system. There were holes in the seat sidecover unit that let you see the carbs and rather than these being extra intakes they serve to let excess air out and enable the mechanics to switch off the fuel taps on the tank.

The spark plugs protruded through the plastic tray, but only just. They were the latest NGKs with only about 10mm of ceramic, shorter even than the special plugs for the three-cylinder Hondas. Their effective length was made shorter still by the fact that the plug-cap connection was made down inside the ceramic. There was no threaded contact

Built for Spencer to win the 250cc World Championship, the little NS250RW was a work of art. With fuel tank removed, this shot shows the braced aluminium frame, twin carburettors and rear suspension mounting.

sticking up on top of the plug. This not only helped with the airflow to the carbs, but meant that the tank could be very low.

The plumbing of the exhaust pipes from the V4 was a real work of art and the 90-degree cylinder split meant that the lower cylinder pipes had to wend their way back and forth under the engine. The upper ones were not so cramped for space as their fattest portions came under the front of the engine. One advantage of the ATAC boxes was that the volume of the pipes themselves could be fractionally less.

The ATAC chamber drive was taken off the right-hand side of the single crank and photos show a small cap over the ATAC drive, secured by three screws, in front of the clutch and beneath the water pump housing. At 45 degrees forward of the vertical, a shaft comes out of the engine running up and forward to the upper cylinder exhausts and down and back to the lower boxes.

After building the first NSR500, which one of the team suggested was 'more of a dream than a motorcycle,' Honda then redesigned it and developed the 'four' to the point where at the end of 1985 it was a better all-round racing machine than the three-cylinder NS500. At the same time they also gave Spencer a superb 250.

Honda NS250RW

When Spencer first rode the NS250RW in public at Daytona in March 1985 it caused quite a stir as the engine bore no relationship to any other previous 250 Honda. Rather than being a special works version of the production RS250R racer available to the public, Spencer's Daytona 100-mile race-winning 250 was half a V4. For although it was still a V-twin like the production bike, Spencer's machine had the vee tipped further forward like the NSR500.

The production bike had a carburettor on the back of each cylinder feeding through a reed-valve to the cylinder. The works version fed through reed-valves direct to the crankcases, just like the V4. It had a single-casting, twin-choke carburettor sitting on the top of the gearbox feeding the crankcases, similar to the set-up on the NSR500.

Takeo Fukui, director of Honda Racing Corporation, confirmed that Spencer's twin and the 'four' were part of the same project, shared the same bore and stroke (54mm X 54mm) and had no parts in common with the production 250.

The single, very short, crank had on the right-hand end a gear driving the clutch, the water pump and the ATAC mechanism. The end of the crank was in the middle of the triangle formed by these three units, which made the engine narrower than if the pump or the ATAC drive were on the end.

There was one crankcase side cover that goes round the pump and ATAC drive, but so that the gearbox internals could be changed without disturbing these, there was a large porthole in the rear of this cover behind the clutch. Over this hole went a separate cover that could be removed once the clutch was off and this cover held the gearbox shafts. So that the clutch sat as close into the engine as possible this gearbox cover was deeply recessed.

To give more accurate timing, the ignition rotor was not gear-driven off the crank, but was mounted on the left-hand end of the crank. Above and behind the ignition could be seen the reed-valve box with the raised 'Honda' lettering. Like the NSR500 the 250 had its reed-valve boxes turned through 90 degrees.

The advantage of these crankcase induction engines is that there is far more room for a bigger reed-valve than in the back of the cylinder. It also leaves more room in the cylinder for transfer ports.

Having the two carburettors in one lump helped in another very important way. It made the feeding of cool air to the RW engine far easier than the production bikes with their separate carbs mounted on the back of each cylinder.

The 250 had a similar airbox arrangement to the 500. It is not just the major things that were impressive about the Honda, but the fact that small details had received just as much consideration, right down to the plastic half-cylinders securing the plug caps. They go over the plug cap and under the plug hexagon.

The frame on the NS250RW was also a mirror image of the 500 twin-spar. The tubes

Engine of the NS250RW was in effect half a NSR500 four. This shot, taken from underneath, shows the lower cylinder with the exhaust from the upper cylinder running down beside it.

were not entirely hollow, though, and a close inspection revealed two slight grooves running the length of each spar. These grooves point out the position of cross-pieces within the extrusion so that looking at one open end would reveal three square ovals, one on top of the other rather than one open rectangle.

The two spars ran from the steering head to the swing-arm area, where on each side a machined section supported the rear engine mounts and the swinging-arm pivots. The engine hung on fabricated arms that were welded to the main spars some way to the rear of the steering head. From the point where these engine mounts were welded to the head there was some fabricated triangulation that built up the section and strength of the spars and fully supported the head.

The rear suspension was provided by the classic Honda Pro-Link and featured a connecting-rod running back from the frame to

the lowest point of the rocker. The rear of the rocker pivoted in the swing arm and the front-end was connected to the bottom of the remote-reservoir Showa unit. The 500 was slightly different with the connecting-rod and rocker above the frame, but both functioned in the same manner.

The swing arms were, like the frame, made from extruded-section aluminium and a carbon-fibre rear disc was used. The front top-quarter of the rear wheel was enclosed by a fairing that cut turbulence and hence drag. More might ideally be covered, but this is not allowed under FIM regulations.

The tyres used were the Michelin radials, which can be given some credit for the success of Spencer and the Honda. The World Champion had the advantage of the bike and tyres being developed together for his needs. More than that, the 250 equipment was developed alongside the 500 so that as far as possible swapping from one machine to the other required the least adaptation.

The 250 in fact preceded the 500 and was tested at Surfers Paradise, in Australia, in December 1984. So impressed was Spencer with the 250 that he simply asked for a 500 just like a big brother to the little twin. That is what he got and both bikes were developed side-by-side, and although he pointed out that there were obvious difference between riding the two bikes, because of the sheer power involved, there were instances where running two machines had been an advantage: 'The most obvious is where it has been wet because racing one bike on the circuit has given me a good idea how much traction there is when it comes to the other. The 250 is quite often faster round a certain corner in the wet because the 500 has to be turned sooner if you want to get the power

on. Even in the dry there are sections where I am quicker on the 250. The secret with the smaller bike is keeping the momentum up round the turns because it doesn't have the power to drive out.'

Spencer pointed out that the 250 had been more fun to ride than the 500: 'You cannot say the 500 is fun to ride, although it is very satisfying if you get things right. Early in the year it was hard on the 500 because the handling was not right. I couldn't use the radial front because I had chattering problems and I didn't race with it until Mugello. By that time the engine of the 500 had been moved forward, which made it possible to get the suspension right and let the tyre work. With the 250 it has never been a problem to use the radial, and that made things better from the beginning. Although it is harder to run a consistently fast

Typical practice day scene as Spencer waits while mechanics ready his NS250RW Honda.

The NS250RW with the streamlining off at the 1985 Belgian Grand Prix.

race all the way through with the 500 because of the sheer physical effort required, the 250 is in fact more intense as far as competition goes even if, physically, it is more relaxed and I am able to loosen up a bit.'

Variety the spice of life

The V-twin and V4 Grand Prix two-strokes may have been the most refined machines Spencer has ridden, but even while pursuing the World Championships he still had to ride the big four-strokes on occasion, including outings on the VF750-based Superbike and the monstrous FWS1000 (also known as the RS1000RW) that he raced at Daytona at the beginning of 1982. That machine had no real connection with any road machine and proved almost too powerful and heavy. That Daytona was typical, as Spencer suffered tyre failures because the machine was just too much for the rubber available.

Mike Baldwin won the American Formula One Championship on the machine, even though the AMA removed the restrictor rule from the 750s because the Honda was so fast at Daytona. Spencer only returned from Europe to ride at Laguna Seca and then he brought the NS500 with him and the 500s proved to be much better racing machines than the big water-cooled V4 four-stroke.

In 1983 Honda had another V4 to play with when the Superbike regulations changed to a maximum of 750cc and they employed their VF750 road bike. Spencer raced it at Daytona and the watercooled four-valves-per-cylinder machine proved very competitive; Spencer led a Honda clean sweep that March.

Just as they had for the old across-the-frame, air-cooled 'four', Honda produced a race kit for the V4. It included a dry clutch, exhaust pipes, oil-coolers, ignition system, magnesium Keihin carbs and, very importantly, a gear cam-drive conversion that replaced the more fragile chain.

Spencer made it a hat-trick of Daytona

Muscle machine. This is the incredible 750cc V4 Honda four-stroke that Freddie rode to victory in the Superbike 100-miler at Daytona in 1984 – a far cry from the tiny NS250RW of 1985!

After three years of racing only in the 500cc class, the 250 presented new problems. Left Freddie and Erv Kanemoto think things over at the French Grand Prix in 1985. Kanemoto, above, is Honda team manager and Spencer's long-time technical advisor.

Superbike wins by repeating the performance in 1984 and 1985. Honda continued to improve the machine and great deal of work was done by Udo Geitl and his team in America who were eventually claiming some 130bhp at 12,000rpm. The road bike forks of the old Superbike were long gone and Showa made special 41.3mm racing forks and a rear suspension unit to go with the Pro-Link rear linkage. The swing arms were fabricated from extruded sections and replaced the standard cast units.

So Spencer has won races on every kind of modern racing machine on which he has seriously competed: four-cylinder four-strokes; four, three and twin-cylinder two-strokes – it has mattered little. He says he finds the 250 twin more fun, but the enjoyment, or lack of it, that Spencer feels has never affected the true professionalism with which he rides his machines.

In fact it is the challenge that goes with swapping from one racing motorcycle to another that Spencer relishes. He was doing that at Daytona in 1985 almost as frequently as he used to as a club racer back in 1977 when he won four Western Road Race Association National Championships. At the time he rode an amazing number of machines including a 125cc Honda for the 200cc GP class, two almost identical RD400 Yamahas for the 400cc Production classes, a 750cc Suzuki and a TZ250 Yamaha; and he was only 15!

'I used to ride 10 races in a day, I'd get off the 750 and go out on the 125 without even taking my helmet off. I loved the challenge and the variety and I guess I still do.'

Soon after clinching the 500cc title in Sweden, Freddie poses with his two World Championship winning machines — the NS250RW (left) and the NSR500.